Handmade Gifts
FROM THE KITCHEN

Handmade Gifts
FROM THE KITCHEN

More than 100 culinary inspired presents to make and bake

ALISON WALKER

Photography by
Tara Fisher

appetite
by RANDOM HOUSE

Appetite by Random House edition
published 2014

Library and Archives of Canada Cataloguing
in Publication is available upon request

ISBN: 978-0-449-01667-1
eBook ISBN: 978-0-449-01668-8

Printed and bound in China

Published in Canada by Appetite by Random
House®, a division of Random House of
Canada Limited, a Penguin Random House
Company

www.randomhouse.ca

10 9 8 7 6 5 4 3 2 1

Managing Editor: **Lydia Halliday**
Photographer: **Tara Fisher**
Art Director and Designer: **Penny Stock**
Design Concept: **Laura Woussen**
Project Manager and Editor: **Nikki Sims**
Prop Stylist: **Caroline Reeves**
Production: **Maeve Healy**

Oven temperatures are for conventional
ovens, for convection ovens please reduce
the temperature by 68°F accordingly.

Contents

INTRODUCTION

I love to cook, and spend as much time in my kitchen as possible. But it's not just the act of cooking itself that fills me with joy. The true pleasure comes from sharing food that I've made for family and friends. A sweet or savory homemade gift, thoughtfully created for someone special will always be more appreciated than any store-bought version.

Throughout the year, I stock my pantry with seasonal treats, such as jellies, chutneys, and liqueurs, that make wonderful impromptu gifts—and something more interesting to take to a dinner party than a bottle of wine! Any festive occasion is the perfect excuse for me to rustle up cakes, bread, or batches of candies, whether it's Thanksgiving, Easter, or Valentine's Day. At Christmas time, I pack gift bags with an assortment of goodies that are handed to guests as they leave.

You'll find all sorts of recipes in this book—from simple things to make with children, such as the tiffin and chocolate mendiants, to savory crackers and chutney that can be paired with a favorite cheese to truly impressive and glamorous macarons and truffles displayed in pretty boxes tied with a luxurious ribbon. I haven't forgotten gifts for the cooks themselves, either, with ideas for Italian temptations and a whole gingerbread house to build and decorate among others.

Why make rather than buy? Well, most of the time it's much cheaper than buying something from a store, it's a good way to use up any garden gluts, you know exactly what has gone into it, it's a pleasure for the cook as well as the recipient, and, above all, it's a gift made with love. And what could be better than that?

Alison

Baked
with love

SPICED STARS

PREPARATION: *35 minutes,*
  plus chilling
COOKING: *8 minutes*
MAKES: *about 40*

1 stick butter, plus extra for
  greasing
scant ¼ cup molasses
seeds from 4 green cardamom
  pods, crushed
¼ tsp freshly ground black
  pepper

scant ¼ cup superfine sugar
1 tbsp almond flour
1½ cups plus 1 tbsp all-purpose
  flour
½ tsp baking soda
½ tsp ground allspice
1 egg yolk, beaten

TO DECORATE (OPTIONAL):
royal icing (about 7oz)
superfine sugar, for sprinkling

I think that Scandinavians do spice really well, and these Scandi-style cookies are flavored with aromatic cardamom and black pepper. I find the flavor improves with keeping, so it's a good idea to make these the week before giving your gift.

1 Melt the butter and molasses in a pan on a gentle heat. Cool a little.
2 In a large bowl mix all of the dry ingredients together and make a well in the center. Pour in the molasses mixture followed by the egg yolk. Mix to form a soft dough and then wrap in plastic wrap—it will be very soft but don't worry. Chill for at least an hour until the dough is firm but still pliable. Meanwhile, preheat the oven to 375°F, and lightly grease two to three cookie sheets.
3 Remove the dough from the refrigerator, divide it in two, and roll out each piece on a lightly floured counter to ¼-inch thick. Using 2¾-inch and 2-inch star-shaped cutters, stamp out shapes, re-rolling the trimmings as necessary. Arrange the star shapes on the cookie sheets, spacing them apart.
4 Bake in a preheated oven for 6 to 8 minutes.
5 Remove from the oven and let cool for 5 minutes on the cookie sheets until set, then transfer to wire racks to cool.
6 If you'd like to decorate your stars, fill a pastry bag with royal icing and pipe shapes onto the cookies. While the icing is still wet, dust lightly with superfine sugar, shaking off the excess. Let dry completely, before packing in cellophane. These cookies keep for up to four weeks in an airtight container or sealed plastic bag.

CHERRY AND ALMOND BISCOTTI

PREPARATION: *35 minutes*
COOKING: *1 hour 5 minutes*
MAKES: *about 60*

2 cups 00 Italian flour
¼ tsp baking powder
1 cup golden superfine sugar
2 large eggs, beaten with 1 tsp
almond extract
finely grated zest 1 lemon
¾ cup blanched almonds,
toasted and roughly chopped
⅔ cup dried cherries

I find these moreish Italian cookies are perfect partners to a glass of Vin Santo or an after-dinner espresso.

1 Preheat the oven to 400°F. Lightly grease a large cookie sheet; you'll need a couple more later on.
2 Sift the flour onto a counter with the baking powder, then make a large well in the center, by pushing the flour to the edge.
3 Put the sugar, eggs, and lemon zest in the center and gradually work in the flour with the fingertips of one hand. (You could do this in a bowl, beating the eggs and sugar together before adding the flour, but the messy method is more fun and actually easier to do.)
4 When the eggs and sugar are thoroughly incorporated, knead in the almonds and cherries.
5 Divide the finished dough into two pieces and shape each into a "sausage" about 12 inches long and transfer to the cookie sheet. Flatten slightly, so that it is about 1¼ inches high. Bake for 20 minutes until set and lightly golden.
6 Remove from the oven and cool for a few minutes on a wire rack. Turn down the oven temperature to 300°F.
7 Using a serrated knife, slice each biscotti "sausage" slightly on the angle at ½-inch intervals. Arrange the biscotti in one layer on two or three cookie sheets. Bake for 40 to 45 minutes until dried out.
8 Remove from the oven and cool on wire racks. These crunchy biscotti keep for two months in an airtight container or sealed plastic bag.

CHOCOLATE SHORTBREAD BUTTONS

PREPARATION: *20 minutes,*
   plus chilling
COOKING: *20 minutes*
MAKES: *18 to 20*

¾ cup unsalted butter, softened
6 tbsp superfine sugar
1 tsp vanilla extract
1¼ cups all-purpose flour, plus
   extra for dusting
½ cup rice flour
scant 2 tbsp unsweetened cocoa
   powder
a pinch of salt

This is a modern take on the classic shortbread circles, this time with added chocolate and in a cute button shape; the plain version is equally delicious*. Threading the holes with colored twine is a fun touch.

1 Preheat the oven to 325°F, and then line two cookie sheets with parchment paper.
2 Cream the butter and sugar together with an electric mixer until soft and fluffy and almost white in color, then beat in the vanilla extract.
3 Sift together the flours and cocoa powder with the salt, then add to the butter mixture. Blend with a fork to form a dough.
4 Knead on a very lightly floured counter (be wary of the fact that too much flour will make the cookies dry) until smooth. Flatten into a disc, wrap in plastic wrap, and chill for 30 minutes.
5 Take out of the refrigerator and on a lightly floured counter roll out the dough to a ¼-inch thickness. Cut out circles with a plain 2½-inch cutter. Using a 2-inch plain cutter, press just inside the cookie almost halfway through. With a skewer, make four small holes in the center to represent button holes. Arrange on the sheets and chill for 30 minutes.
6 Bake for 10 to 15 minutes until just firm. If the button markings have blurred during baking, gently re-mark with the cutter and skewer while still warm and pliable. Let cool for 1 to 2 minutes on the sheets before transferring to a wire rack to cool. These cookies keep for four weeks in an airtight container or sealed plastic bag.
* To make the plain shortbread version, simply omit the cocoa powder and use 1⅓ cups of plain flour instead.

VIENNESE WHIRLS

PREPARATION: *30 minutes*
COOKING: *12 minutes*
MAKES: *15 to 20*

1 stick plus 1 tbsp unsalted
  butter, very soft, plus extra for
  greasing
¼ cup confectioners' sugar,
  sifted
scant 1 cup self-rising flour
½ tsp vanilla bean paste

These melt-in-the-mouth cookies work well in all manner of shapes. I like this classic whirl, or "S" shape—but you could make fingers or flowers simply by piping the mixture into those shapes before you bake them. Alternatively, transform two cookies into a Viennese sandwich with a layer of flavored buttercream or dip the ends in melted chocolate. These gifts work equally well as a petit four or served with a bowl of ice cream; something to put on the label, perhaps.

1 Preheat the oven to 375°F. Lightly grease one or two large cookie sheets.
2 Beat the butter and confectioners' sugar with an electric mixer until light and fluffy and almost white in color. Beat in the vanilla bean paste.
3 Using a fork, blend the flour and baking powder into the butter in three batches, until smooth.
4 Fit a pastry bag with a ¾-inch star tip and fill with the cookie mixture. Pipe "S" shapes on to the cookie sheets about 2½ to 2¾ inches long and space them well apart. (If the mixture becomes over-soft while piping, chill the bag for a few minutes before resuming.)
5 Bake in a preheated oven for 10 to 12 minutes until lightly golden at the edges. Remove from the oven and transfer to a wire rack to cool. These keep for four weeks in an airtight container or sealed plastic bag.

LAVENDER MADELEINES

PREPARATION: *25 minutes,*
  plus standing
COOKING: *10 minutes*
MAKES: *18*

*scant ½ cup lavender sugar**
2 medium eggs
¾ cup all-purpose flour, plus
  extra for dusting
¾ tsp baking powder
1 stick butter, melted, plus extra
  for greasing

These buttery French cakes are instantly recognizable by their pretty scalloped shell shape. Dust with confectioners' sugar or give with some chocolate fudge sauce (see page 111) for dipping them into.

1 Preheat the oven to 400°F. Brush a Madeleine pan with melted butter and a good dusting of flour. Tap out the excess.
2 Beat the sugar and eggs until light and fluffy. Fold in the flour and baking powder, followed by the butter. Let stand for 30 minutes.
3 Fill each mold three-quarters full of the batter and bake in a preheated oven for 8 to 10 minutes until golden and risen. Remove from the oven, let cool for a few minutes, and transfer to a wire rack.
4 These cakes keep for two to three days in an airtight container or sealed plastic bag but are best eaten on the day they're made.
(* To make lavender sugar, put a handful of lavender flower sprigs into a container of superfine sugar. Seal and leave for at least two weeks for the flavour to infuse before using.)

EARL GREY HEARTS

A gently flavored cookie that could be gifted to tea lovers with
a packet of their favorite brew.

PREPARATION: *35 minutes,*
  plus chilling
COOKING: *10 minutes*
MAKES: *25 to 30*

scant 1½ cups all-purpose flour
scant ½ cup confectioners' sugar
1 tsp Earl Grey tea
1 stick butter, softened, plus extra
  for greasing
1 medium egg yolk

1 Put the flour, confectioners' sugar, and tea into a food processor. Add
the rest of the ingredients and whiz to form a soft dough. Shape into a
disc, wrap in plastic wrap, and chill for 20 minutes.
2 Meanwhile, preheat the oven to 375°F, and lightly grease two to three
cookie sheets.
3 Remove the dough from the refrigerator and lightly flour a counter.
Roll out to a ¼-inch thickness, cut out shapes with a 2-inch heart-
shaped cutter, and space apart on the cookie sheets.
4 Bake in a preheated oven for 8 to 10 minutes until lightly golden. Let
cool on the sheets for a couple of minutes before transferring to wire
racks to cool completely. These cookies keep for up to four weeks in
an airtight container or sealed plastic bag.

STOLLEN WREATH

PREPARATION: *45 minutes,*
  plus macerating and rising
COOKING: *40 minutes*
SERVES: **10 to 12**

⅔ cup each of raisins and golden
  raisins
2 tbsp rum
7 tsp active dry yeast (or ¼ cup
  fresh yeast)
scant ½ cup lukewarm milk
3 cups white bread flour
¼ tsp ground coriander
a grating of fresh nutmeg
¼ cup superfine sugar
1 tsp salt
1 stick plus 1 tbsp soft butter,
  diced
1 medium egg
sunflower oil, for greasing
3 tbsp candied peel
2 tbsp blanched almonds, split
  lengthwise
finely grated zest of 1 lemon
⅓ cup unsalted butter, melted
confectioners' sugar, for dusting

Stollen is traditionally shaped into a flat loaf but here I've opted for a wreath—it would make a stunning centerpiece for a Christmas table.

1 Put the dried fruit into a non-metallic bowl with the rum. Let stand overnight.

2 Mix together the yeast and milk then stir in ¾ cup of the flour. Cover and let stand for 2 hours—the mixture should bubble.

3 Mix together the remaining flour with the spices, sugar, and salt. Make a well in the center and add the butter, egg, and the yeast mixture. Bring together with your hands—don't worry, it will seem crumbly to start with but that will change once you start kneading.

4 Turn out onto a counter and knead until smooth and elastic—as the butter is worked into the dough it will become smoother. (Alternatively, use the dough hook attachment on a stand mixer and mix for 2 minutes at the lowest speed, then 5 to 7 minutes on medium speed until the dough is stretchy and elastic.) Turn into a lightly oiled bowl, cover with plastic wrap and let rise for 2 hours till doubled in size.

4 Turn out the dough onto a lightly floured counter and press out flat into a rectangle 15¾ inches x 11 inches. Sprinkle with the soaked dried fruit, candied peel, almonds, and lemon zest. From one long end, roll up the dough into a jelly roll shape. Cut in half lengthwise, carefully turn the cut sides uppermost, then braid like a rope. Transfer to a greased cookie sheet and shape into a ring, twisting the two ends together and tucking underneath to hide the join. Cover loosely with oiled plastic wrap, and let proof for an hour until doubled in size.

5 Preheat the oven to 350°F. Bake for 35 to 40 minutes; when it's ready, the bottom should sound hollow when tapped. Remove from the oven and cool on a wire rack for 20 minutes, then brush the top and sides with the melted butter, allowing each coat to dry for a few seconds before adding the next one.

6 Just before serving or wrapping, dust heavily with confectioners' sugar. This sweet bread keeps for up to a week in an airtight container.

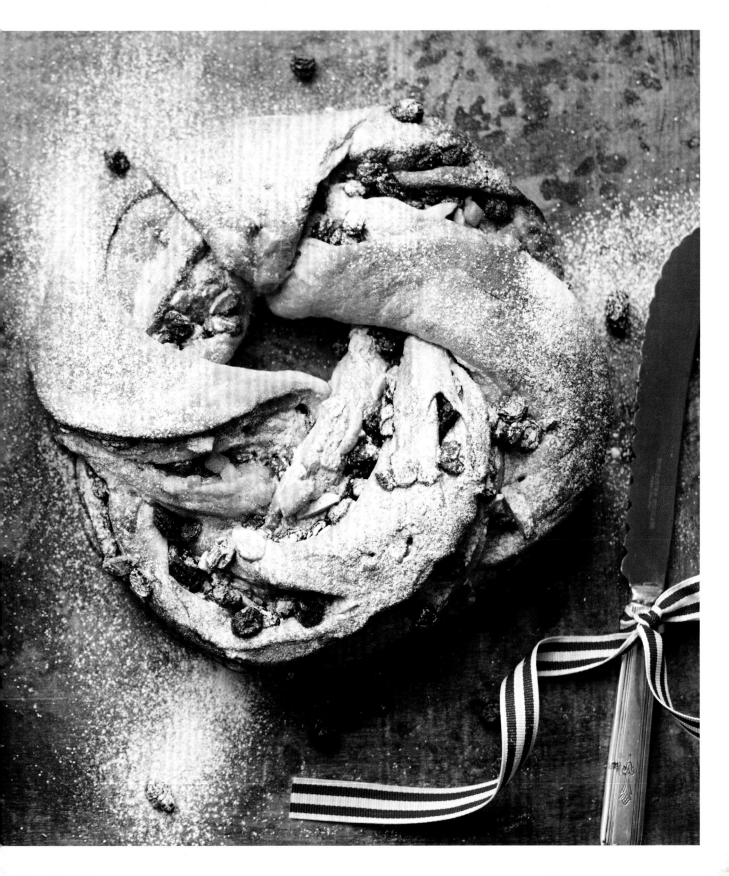

FONDANT CUPCAKES

PREPARATION: *40 minutes*
COOKING: *15 minutes*
MAKES: 18

FOR THE CUPCAKES:
*scant 1 cup golden superfine
  sugar*
*2 sticks unsalted butter, very
  soft*
*finely grated zest and juice of
  1 lemon*
1–2 tbsp lukewarm water
4 medium eggs, beaten
1¾ cups self-rising flour

FOR THE FONDANT:
*6 cups fondant confectioners'
  sugar, sifted*
2 tbsp lemon juice
*crystallized flowers, to decorate
  (see right)*

These adorable cupcakes can be adapted to suit any occasion. Tint the icing palest pink for Valentine's Day and decorate with rose petals or embellish with primroses for Mother's Day.

1 Preheat the oven to 400°F. Line two 12-hole muffin tins with 18 cupcake liners.
2 Put the cupcake ingredients into a large bowl and beat with an electric mixer for 2 minutes until fluffy and paler in color.
3 Divide the mixture equally among the cupcake liners and bake in a preheated oven for 12 to 15 minutes until golden. Remove from the oven and transfer to a wire rack to cool. These cakes should have fairly flat tops that rise to just below the top of the paper liner (to allow for the fondant) but trim if necessary before pouring in the fondant.
4 To make the fondant, put the confectioners' sugar in a large bowl. Gradually beat in the lemon juice and the water, as necessary, until you have a soft but spreadable consistency that holds its shape.
5 When the cakes are completely cold, flood the fondant on top of the cakes up to the edges of the cupcake liners. Let set without moving. When almost set and still slightly wet, decorate with crystallized flowers.

MAKE YOUR OWN CRYSTALLIZED FLOWERS
You can crystallize a variety of flowers and herbs as long as they are edible. My favorites are rose buds and petals, violets, primroses, lavender, mint, rosemary, and sweet geranium leaves. Make sure they are unsprayed.
To make crystallized flowers, lightly beat one large egg white until lightly frothy. Using a small paintbrush, coat the petals or bud with a little of the egg white. Let dry for a few seconds, then sprinkle with superfine sugar—this is important because the sugar will become wet and sticky if sprinkled on too quickly. Set on parchment paper to dry—ideally in an airing cupboard or somewhere warm. Such crystallized flowers will keep in an airtight container for up to a week in a cool, dry place.

MACARONS

PREPARATION: *1 hour, plus*
  resting
COOKING: *15 minutes*
MAKES: *20*

generous ⅓ cup egg whites
1 cup almond flour
1½ cups confectioners' sugar
3 tbsp superfine sugar
¼ tsp vanilla extract
yellow food coloring paste
4 tbsp good-quality store-bought
  lemon curd

1 The day before you make the macarons, separate the eggs and put the whites in a bowl loosely covered in the refrigerator.

2 When you are ready to make the macarons, bring the egg whites to room temperature. Draw 1½-inch circles at spaced intervals on two to three sheets of parchment paper as a template to guide your piping. Turn it over and use this parchment to line two to three cookie sheets.

3 Put the almond flour and confectioners' sugar in a food processor and whiz until they become a fine powder. Sieve three times to remove any lumps of almond—this ensures a smooth surface to your macarons.

4 Beat the egg whites to a medium peak, then beat in the superfine sugar. Next, beat in the vanilla extract and food coloring—be generous with the coloring paste as it fades during baking.

5 Using a spatula, fold the almond mixture into the egg whites in two batches—it should be a fairly fluid batter but still be able to be piped.

6 Dot blobs of this batter on to the underside of each corner of parchment to keep it still during cooking. Transfer the mixture to a pastry bag fitted with a large plain tip and pipe mounds of the mixture just within the circles. Tap each tray on the counter a couple of times to remove any air bubbles and let stand for anything from 30 minutes to 4 hours, depending on humidity, until the surface of the macarons is no longer tacky—again this is crucial to ensure the macarons have their characteristic frilled feet.

7 Meanwhile, preheat the oven to 325°F. Bake the macarons in a preheated oven for 10 to 15 minutes until they just peel away from the paper when tested. Remove from the oven and immediately slide the parchment paper with the macarons onto a damp counter—this will stop them cooking further and also make them easier to remove.

8 Sandwich two shells together with a blob of lemon curd. These macarons keep for up to a week in the refrigerator. The unfilled shells can be frozen for up to a month.

These elegant treats are sure to elicit "oohs" and "aaahs" on their arrival in a box or on a platter. Do make them when you have no other time pressure—they're not difficult to make but they do need to sit for a while ahead of baking to give them that slightly chewy outside. And don't make them on a rainy day, as they never work!

BAKLAVA

PREPARATION: *35 minutes,*
  plus cooling
COOKING: *1 hour 40 minutes*
MAKES: *about 60 pieces*

4¾ cups walnuts
scant ⅓ cup superfine sugar
¼ tsp ground cinnamon
a pinch of ground cloves
9oz ready-made phyllo dough
1 stick plus 1 tbsp butter, melted

FOR THE SYRUP:
1¼ cups superfine sugar
scant ⅔ cups water
1 whole clove
finely grated zest of 1 lemon
  (I use unwaxed lemons)
2 tbsp liquid honey

This intensely sweet pastry is so versatile—I've made it with hazelnuts and pistachios instead of the walnuts or flavored the syrup with rose water or orange-flower water, all with outstanding results.

1 Preheat the oven to 325°F. Toast the walnuts in a preheated oven for 5 to 10 minutes until golden. Tip onto a plate to cool.
2 Coarsely grind the cooled walnuts in a food processor. Tip into a bowl and stir in the sugar and the spices.
3 Cut the phyllo sheets to the same size as an 11-inch x 7-inch baking pan and cover with a damp dish towel while you're working to stop the sheets drying out.
4 Brush the base and sides of the pan with melted butter. Lay a phyllo sheet in the base, brush with butter, and lay another sheet on top. Repeat with 8 more sheets, brushing in between with butter as you go.
5 Next, spread with one-third of the walnut mixture. Lay another two phyllo sheets on top, buttering as before. Repeat this twice more with the remaining walnut mixture.
6 Lay another 6 sheets of phyllo on top, again brushing each sheet with butter. Brush the top sheet with butter and mark into diamond shapes. Bake for 1½ hours until golden.
7 Meanwhile, make the syrup. Dissolve the sugar in the water with the clove and lemon zest. Bring to the boil then simmer rapidly for 10 minutes until lightly syrupy. Strain and stir in the honey.
8 Remove the baklava from the oven and immediately pour over half of the syrup. Leave for 30 minutes then slowly pour over the remainder. Leave overnight to infuse but do not chill.
9 Cut the baklava into diamond shapes using the previous markings as a guide. This sticky pastry keeps for up to two weeks in an airtight container or sealed plastic bag.

BILLIONAIRE'S SHORTBREAD

PREPARATION: *35 minutes,*
  plus setting
COOKING: *40 minutes*
MAKES: *about 25*

FOR THE SHORTBREAD BASE:
1 cup all-purpose flour, sifted
⅓ cup rice flour
scant ⅓ cup superfine sugar
1 stick plus 1 tbsp unsalted butter,
  diced, plus extra for greasing

FOR THE SALTED CARAMEL:
1 can (14oz) sweetened condensed
  milk
¾ cup soft dark brown sugar
⅔ cup unsalted butter
½ tsp fine sea salt

FOR THE TOPPING:
3½oz semisweet chocolate, broken
  into pieces
3½oz milk chocolate, broken into
  pieces
gold powder, for dusting

1 Preheat the oven to 350°F, and lightly grease a 13-inch x 9-inch baking pan.

2 Sift the flours into a large bowl and stir in the sugar. Rub in the butter until the mixture is crumbly and the fat is evenly distributed.

3 Press the shortbread mixture into the base of the prepared pan. Bake for 20 to 30 minutes until it feels firm to the touch and looks lightly golden. Remove from the oven and set aside on a wire rack to cool.

4 To make the caramel topping, put the condensed milk, sugar, and butter into a heavy-bottom pan and melt over low heat to dissolve the sugar. Bring to a gentle boil for about 5 minutes until thickened. Stir in the salt. Pour over the shortbread base and leave in a cool place to set.

5 Put the chocolate in separate heatproof bowls and set over pans of gently simmering water to melt. Stir once or twice until smooth. Pour random pools of the semisweet chocolate onto the caramel. Fill any gaps with the melted milk chocolate. Using the end of a skewer, swirl the chocolates together to make a pattern. Let set at room temperature. Dust with gold powder using a small paintbrush.

6 Cut into bite-sized squares and lightly dust with gold powder. This shortbread keeps for up to a week in an airtight container.

I've ramped up the classic millionaire's shortbread to the next level here by using a salted caramel filling and a luxurious dusting of gold powder.

WEDDING COOKIES

PREPARATION: *30 minutes,*
  plus chilling
COOKING: **15 minutes**
MAKES: **25 to 30**

½ *cup toasted mixed nuts*
2⅓ *cups all-purpose flour*
2 *sticks unsalted butter, very*
  soft
¼ *cup confectioners' sugar*
½ *tsp anise flavoring*
¼ *tsp salt*
confectioners' sugar,
  for dusting

1 Put the nuts in a food processor with 2 tablespoons of flour and whiz until finely ground—don't overprocess or they will become oily.

2 In a separate bowl, beat together the butter and confectioners' sugar with an electric mixer until light and fluffy. Beat in the anise flavoring.

3 Next, beat in the remaining flour and salt until just combined, followed by the blitzed nuts. Chill for 30 minutes or so until firm.

4 Preheat the oven to 350°F, and then line two cookie sheets with parchment paper.

5 Roll pieces of the dough into walnut-sized balls, flatten slightly and arrange on the cookie sheets 2 inches apart.

6 Bake in a preheated oven for 12 to 15 minutes until lightly golden.

7 Remove from the oven and cool on a wire rack. Dredge with sifted confectioners' sugar and package in cellophane or in boxes.

Looking like miniature snowballs, these delightful cookies were once part of tea-sharing ceremonies in Russia during the 18th century and are now often given out as part of wedding celebrations.

Edible flowers are things of beauty in their own right, so I love to use their subtle tastes to enhance the flavor of baking as well as adding to the esthetics of the finished result. These cookies are real stunners.

ROSE PETAL COOKIES

PREPARATION: *35 minutes,*
  plus chilling
COOKING: *10 minutes*
MAKES: *40 to 50*

1 cup confectioners' sugar, sifted
2 cups all-purpose flour, sifted
2¼ sticks cold butter, diced
2 tbsp unsprayed red rose
  petals, cut into small pieces
  (I use scissors) with white
  heels removed
finely grated zest of 1 lemon

1 Put the sugar, flour, and butter into the bowl of a food processor. Whiz until the mixture resembles fine bread crumbs, then pulse in the rose petals and lemon zest, and transfer to a large bowl.

2 Bring it together with your fingers, then lightly knead until smooth.

3 Preheat the oven to 325°F, and then line two cookie sheets with parchment paper.

4 Take walnut-sized pieces of the cookie dough and roll into balls between your palms. Put the dough balls on the cookie sheets and press down lightly with a fork to flatten them. Bake in a preheated oven for 10 to 12 minutes until lightly golden and set.

5 Remove from the oven and let cool for a couple of minutes on the cookie sheets, then transfer to wire racks to cool. These cookies keep for up to a month in an airtight container or sealed plastic bag.

candies and confections

HOKEY POKEY

PREPARATION: **25 minutes,
plus setting**
COOKING: **10 minutes**
MAKES: **12oz**

4 tbsp corn syrup

scant 1 cup granulated sugar

*3 tbsp unsalted butter, plus
extra for greasing*

2 tbsp water

2 tsp baking soda

½ tsp white wine vinegar

*melted chocolate, for dipping
(optional)*

This recipe brings out the child in me: I still love watching the mixture
fizz and bubble—volcano-like—as the baking soda reacts with the hot
sugar syrup to make this wonderful honeycomb.

1 Grease an 11-inch x 7-inch baking pan. Make sure you can leave it
somewhere undisturbed as you don't want to move it until the hokey
pokey is completely set.

2 Heat the syrup, sugar, and butter in a deep, heavy-bottom pan until
the sugar is dissolved. Using a wet pastry brush, wash down the sides
of the pan to dissolve any stray sugar crystals that may cause the sugar
syrup to crystallize while cooking.

3 Bring the sugar mixture to the boil and boil steadily until a candy
thermometer reads 280°F (the soft crack stage). If you don't have a
thermometer, drop a teaspoon of the mix into a bowl of cold water. Bring
it together with your fingers—it should form firm but pliable threads.

4 Take off the heat and immediately stir in the baking soda followed by
the vinegar—it will fizz and bubble up, so take care.

5 Quickly turn into the prepared pan, pouring in one layer from the top
to the bottom of the pan—don't be tempted to smooth out with a spoon
or shake the pan to level the mixture because this will burst all the
precious bubbles you have just created. Leave to set without moving.

6 Break into pieces and dip into melted chocolate, if you like. These
treats start to get sticky after a couple of days but will keep for up to two
weeks if completely covered in chocolate.

POPCORN BARK

PREPARATION: *30 minutes*
COOKING: *15 minutes*
MAKES: *36 pieces*

1 tbsp sunflower oil, plus extra
   for greasing
½ cup popping corn
1¼ cups dry unsweetened
   coconut
2 cups mini marshmallows
½ cup corn syrup
scant 1 cup granulated sugar
3 tbsp unsalted butter

For some reason, this sticky, chewy treat tastes especially good around a fall campfire—maybe it's something to do with the marshmallows combined with the smells in the air...

1 First, cook the popping corn in batches. Heat half the oil in a deep pan over a medium heat. Add half the popcorn kernels, cover with a tight-fitting lid, and cook until the kernels start popping. Turn off the heat but leave the pan on the burner and shake occasionally until the kernels stop popping. Pour into a large bowl and set aside to cool. Repeat with the remaining oil and popping corn.
2 When the popcorn has cooled, stir in the coconut and marshmallows. Lightly oil a 13-inch x 9-inch baking pan.
3 In a heavy-bottom pan, melt the corn syrup, sugar, and butter over gentle heat until the sugar has dissolved. Using a wet pastry brush, wash down the sides of the pan to dissolve stray sugar crystals that may cause the syrup to crystallize while cooking.
4 Turn up the heat to a steady boil and cook for 4 to 5 minutes until a candy thermometer measures 250°F (the firm ball stage). If you don't have a thermometer, drop a teaspoon of mixture into a bowl of cold water. It should form a firm ball between your fingers.
5 Quickly stir the syrup into the popcorn mixture and immediately turn out into the baking pan—some of the marshmallows will melt and some will stay whole. Level the mixture and leave to set.
6 Turn out the whole bark onto a board lined with parchment paper and then use a sharp knife to cut it into squares. This bark keeps for up to a week in an airtight container or sealed plastic bag.

MARZIPAN ALLSORTS

PREPARATION: *55 minutes*
COOKING: *15 minutes*
MAKES: *30 to 35*

2 cups preserving sugar
scant ⅔ cup water
¼ tsp cream of tartar
3½ cups almond flour
2 medium egg whites, lightly beaten

TO FINISH:
food coloring pastes
confectioners' sugar, for dusting
lightly beaten egg white

A twist on the multilayered licorice allsort, these candies give you a fantastic excuse to play around and create all sorts of multicolored delights. Once you've mastered making your own marzipan, you can use it to model shapes and cover a mini Christmas cake (see page 142).

1 Put the sugar in a large heavy-bottom pan with the water. Heat gently to dissolve the sugar, then bring to a boil. Add the cream of tartar and boil steadily without stirring until a candy thermometer reaches 241°F (the soft ball stage). If you don't have a thermometer, drop a teaspoon of the mixture into a bowl of cold water. Bring it together with your fingers—it should form a soft ball.
2 Take the pan straight off the heat and dip the base in cold water and stir the syrup rapidly until the syrup starts to crystallize or cloud. Stir in the almond flour and egg whites, and cook for about 3 minutes over low heat, stirring continuously.
3 Divide this marzipan mixture equally among three bowls and add your chosen colors with a cocktail stick, stirring them in vigorously with a wooden spoon. Be brave with the amount of food coloring as you want them to look vibrant and eye catching.
4 Spread the marzipan out onto plates or a marble slab until cool enough to handle. Dust a counter with confectioners' sugar and knead the marzipan until smooth and pliable, and to make the color more even. Wrap each portion in parchment paper and leave until cold.
5 Roll each piece into a rectangle roughly 8 inches x 6 inches. Brush the top of the first sheet with the egg white and carefully lay the next on top. Smooth over gently with the flat of your hands to remove any air bubbles or bumps. Repeat with another coating of egg white and the final layer of colored marzipan.
6 Trim away the uneven edges of the marzipan stack using a serrated knife—you will have to clean it regularly as the paste is quite sticky. Cut the layers lengthways into equal-sized strips, then slice crossways into pieces. Arrange the candies on a large piece of parchment paper and leave to dry until no longer tacky. These allsorts keep for up to three weeks in an airtight container or sealed plastic bag.

PEPPERMINT CANDY CANES

PREPARATION: *50 minutes,
    plus drying*
MAKES: **16**

*3½ cups confectioners' sugar,
    sifted*
1 tsp lemon juice
1 large egg white, lightly beaten
½ tsp peppermint extract
red food coloring paste

Feeling all retro? These minty canes will transport you back to Christmases past. Whether you make them as jolly decorations for a Christmas tree or as a little extra-something to tie on gifts, their arrival always elicits gasps and squeals from children, both big and small.

1 Mix the sugar with the lemon juice and enough egg white to make a stiff paste. Flavor with the peppermint extract.
2 Divide the paste into two pieces. Using a cocktail stick, smear a little red coloring onto one piece, then knead well until the dough is a uniform color.
3 Make walnut-sized balls from both pieces of paste. Roll each ball into a sausage shape and then twist a white and red "sausage" together. Roll lightly so that they stick together and smooth the joins. Cut in half.
4 Bend into a cane shape, trim if necessary, and leave to dry completely on a piece of parchment paper. These candy canes keep for four weeks in an airtight container or sealed plastic bag.

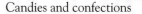

COCONUT ICE

PREPARATION: *25 minutes*
COOKING: *10 minutes*
MAKES: *24 pieces*

sunflower oil, for greasing
4½ cups granulated sugar
1¼ cups whole milk
4 cups dry unsweetened coconut
pink food coloring paste

Cut into whatever sized pieces suit your container or wrap in cellophane and tie with ribbon or butcher's twine.

Many adults will disappear into a moment of nostalgia when greeted with this pink-and-white sweet treat; it's one of the first candies I made as a child, along with peppermint creams. A word of warning about food coloring, though; do be careful when adding the pink color—a dab too far and a pleasant pastel pink can become intensely lurid.

1 Lightly oil an 8-inch square cake pan, and fill the sink or a large basin with cold water.
2 To make the bottom layer, put half of both the sugar and the milk into a heavy-bottom pan and heat gently until the sugar has dissolved. Using a wet pastry brush, wash down the sides of the pan to dissolve any stray sugar crystals that may cause the sugar syrup to crystallize while cooking.
3 Bring the sugar mixture to the boil and boil steadily until a candy thermometer reads 241°F (the soft ball stage). If you don't have a thermometer, drop a teaspoon of the mixture into a bowl of cold water. It should form a soft ball between your fingers.
4 Plunge the base of the pan into cold water to stop the cooking.
5 Quickly stir in half the coconut and turn into the prepared pan.
6 Repeat step 2 with the remaining sugar and milk. Continue as before and then stir in the remaining coconut with a dab of pink food coloring until evenly pink and then pour over the white layer.
7 While it's still soft, mark into bars or squares with a knife. When the coconut ice is completely cold, cut it into the bars. This sweet treat keeps for up to a month in an airtight container or sealed plastic bag so can be made well in advance of giving.

TURKISH DELIGHT

PREPARATION: *20 minutes,*
  plus setting
COOKING: *45 minutes*
MAKES: *36 pieces*

sunflower oil, for greasing
2¼ cups granulated sugar
1 tbsp corn syrup
¾ cup cornstarch
1½ cups plus 1 tbsp
  confectioners' sugar
4 cups water
3 tbsp liquid honey
1 tsp of flavoring (rose water,
  lemon extract, peppermint
  extract, or orange-flower
  water)
a dab of pink, yellow, or green
  food coloring paste
cornstarch and confectioners'
  sugar, for dredging

For some reason, I always think of Turkish delight as an exotic, grown-up treat—probably a combination of the "glamorous" ad that was televised when I was growing up and the fact that my mother always kept it tucked out of reach on a high shelf.

1 Grease an 8-inch square pan (or one of similar dimensions). Fill the sink or a large bowl with cold water.
2 Put the sugar and corn syrup in a large heavy-bottom pan with scant ⅔ cups of the water. Gently heat until the sugar has dissolved. Wash down the sides of the pan with a pastry brush dipped in water to dissolve any sugar crystals.
3 Bring the sugar mixture to the boil and boil steadily until a candy thermometer reads 241°F (the soft ball stage). If you don't have a thermometer, drop a teaspoon of the mixture into a bowl of cold water. Bring it together with your fingers—it should form a soft ball. Plunge the base of the pan into the cold water to stop the syrup cooking.
4 Mix together the cornstarch and confectioners' sugar in a large bowl with scant ½ cup of the water. Bring the remaining water to the boil, then gradually beat into the cornstarch mixture with a wooden spoon.
5 Pour the cornstarch mixture into the pan and simmer until thickened, beating to ensure there are no lumps.
6 Gradually beat in the sugar syrup and simmer rapidly for about 30 to 35 minutes, stirring often, especially towards the end of the cooking time. The mixture should become very thick and turn pale golden.
7 Add the honey, chosen flavoring, and food coloring and stir well. Turn out into the prepared pan and leave in a cool place overnight to set.
8 Lay a sheet of parchment paper on the counter and dust liberally with a mixture of cornstarch and confectioners' sugar. Loosen the edges of the Turkish delight with a knife and turn out onto the parchment. Dust the top again and cut into squares. Toss well in the cornstarch mixture. This Turkish delight keeps for up to two weeks in an airtight container or sealed plastic bag.

RASPBERRY AND VANILLA MARSHMALLOWS

PREPARATION: *25 minutes,*
  plus setting
COOKING: *10 minutes*
MAKES: *60–70 pieces*

FOR THE RASPBERRY JELLO:
gelatin sheets to a weight of 12g
  or ⅓ oz (most sheets weigh 2g
  but check your package)
2 cups raspberries
1 tbsp confectioners' sugar
pink food coloring paste

FOR THE MARSHMALLOW:
sunflower oil, for greasing
3 tbsp confectioners' sugar and
  3 tbsp cornstarch combined, for
  dusting
2¼ cups granulated sugar
1 tbsp corn syrup
generous ¾ cup water
gelatin leaves to a weight of 22g
  or ¾oz
2 medium egg whites
1 tsp vanilla extract

1 Make the raspberry jello. Fill a bowl with cold water and soak the gelatin for 5 minutes. Cook the raspberries gently in a small pan with the confectioners' sugar and a splash of water (they'll release their juices and collapse). Push through a sieve into a bowl and discard the seeds.

2 Rinse the pan and heat the raspberry purée gently. Meanwhile, squeeze the excess water out of the gelatin and melt into the purée.

3 Fill a large bowl with ice and water and set the pan over it. Stir every so often to cool down the mixture—you need it to set enough that it thickens but is still fluid enough to fold into the marshmallow.

4 To make the marshmallows, fill the sink or a large bowl with cold water. Lightly oil a 13-inch x 9-inch pan. Dust the inside with 1 tablespoon each of sifted cornstarch and confectioners' sugar.

5 Over a low heat, melt the granulated sugar with the corn syrup and water until the sugar has completely dissolved. Using a wet pastry brush, wash down the sides of the pan to dissolve any stray sugar crystals that may cause the sugar syrup to crystallize. Meanwhile, put the gelatin sheets into a bowl of cold water to soften, ás before.

6 Bring the syrup to the boil—do not stir—and cook until a candy thermometer measures 261°F (the hard ball stage). If you don't have a thermometer, drop a teaspoon of the mixture into a bowl of cold water. Bring it together with your fingers—it should form a hard ball. When it reaches the correct temperature, plunge the base of the pan into the sink of cold water to stop the syrup cooking.

7 Squeeze out the excess water from the gelatin and stir into the syrup.

8 Just before the sugar syrup reaches the correct temperature, beat the egg whites until stiff, then beat in the vanilla extract briefly. With the beat still running, trickle in the sugar syrup. This is easier with a stand mixer but you could also beat with an electric mixer if you have someone to help pour in the syrup. Beat for about 10 minutes until the mixture holds its shape—it will be a thick white mass. Finally, beat in a few dabs (or drops) of pink food coloring.

9 Swirl in the raspberry purée jello so that it forms ripples. Pour into the prepared pan, smooth out, and leave to set for several hours.

10 Liberally dust a large sheet of parchment paper with the cornstarch and confectioners' sugar mixture. Loosen the marshmallow at the edges with a flat-bladed knife and turn out on to the parchment paper.

11 Dust the top again and leave for 1 hour to form a crust. Cut into squares and toss in the confectioners' sugar. This marshmallow keeps for up to two weeks in an airtight container or sealed plastic bag.

These soft, pillowy marshmallows are rippled with a tangy raspberry jello that looks pretty and tastes divine. Purists might prefer their marshmallow as plain vanilla, in which case simply omit the fruity part.

HONEY AND ALMOND NOUGAT

PREPARATION: *40 minutes,*
  plus standing
COOKING: *15 minutes*
MAKES: *64 pieces*

rice paper sheets
7 tbsp liquid honey
scant 1¼ cups granulated sugar
1 tbsp corn syrup
½ cup water
2 medium egg whites
1 tsp vanilla extract
1 cup almonds, warmed
¾ cup apricots, roughly chopped

This nougat will bring a smile to the face of any recipient as they bite into the wonderfully white gooey chewiness. I like to experiment when making this nougat—each time using a different honey, such as orange blossom, wildflower, or lavender, or varying the nuts to include pistachios or macadamias instead.

1 Line an 8-inch square pan with plastic wrap, overlapping the sides of the pan. Cover the base with rice paper. Keep the honey warm in a small bowl set in a bowl of boiling water from the kettle. Fill the sink or a large bowl with cold water.

2 Put the sugar, glucose, and the water into a medium-sized, heavy-bottom pan and set over a low heat until the sugar has completely dissolved. Bring to a boil, without stirring, and cook until the mixture reaches 280°F on a candy thermometer.

3 Stir in the honey and continue boiling until the temperature reaches 311°F. As it's approaching the critical temperature, beat the egg whites in a stand mixer until stiff, ready for step 4. Once the syrup reaches 311°F, plunge the base of the pan into the sink or a bowl of cold water to stop the syrup cooking further.

4 While the motor of the mixer is running, carefully pour in the syrup in a thin stream into the stiff egg whites. Keep beating until the mixture is thick and holds its shape but is still pourable.

5 Next, beat in the vanilla. Then, fold in the warm nuts and chopped apricots and pour into the pan. Smooth out the top and cover with more rice paper. Fold over the plastic wrap and put another baking pan with weights on top to weigh it down. Leave in a cool place overnight to set.

6 When set, cut into pieces (whatever size you like) and wrap in cellophane. This nougat keeps for up to two weeks in an airtight container or sealed plastic bag.

TREACLE TOFFEE

PREPARATION: *30 minutes,*
  plus setting
COOKING: *20 minutes*
MAKES: *about 2lb*

1 stick unsalted butter, plus
  extra for greasing
2½ cups light brown sugar
generous 6 tbsp corn syrup
scant ⅔ cup cold water
generous 5 tbsp molasses

Hands off kids! This toffee
is strictly for the grown-ups.
The strong, treacley-like flavor
comes from the molasses.

1 Lightly grease a 13-inch x 9-inch baking pan, or one with similar dimensions. Fill the sink or a large bowl with cold water.
2 Put the sugar along with 1 tablespoon of the corn syrup in a large heavy-bottom pan with the water. Gently heat until the sugar has dissolved. Wash down the sides of the pan with a wet pastry brush to dissolve any sugar crystals.
3 When the sugar has completely dissolved, add the remaining ingredients and bring to a boil. Boil steadily without stirring until a candy thermometer reaches 270°F (the soft crack stage). If you don't have a thermometer, drop a teaspoon of the mixture into a bowl of cold water. Bring it together with your fingers—it should form firm but pliable threads. When it reaches the correct temperature, dip the base of the pan into the sink of cold water to stop the syrup cooking.
4 Pour into the prepared pan and leave to cool, marking into squares before it sets. Turn out the toffee when it is completely cold and break into squares. Wrap in colored foil, lined with waxed paper, or cellophane. This toffee keeps for up to a month in a cool place.

VANILLA CARAMELS

PREPARATION: *15 minutes,*
plus setting
COOKING: *20 minutes*
MAKES: *about 1lb 10oz*

sunflower oil, for greasing
2¼ cups granulated sugar
scant ⅔ cup milk
6 tbsp corn syrup
7oz canned sweetened condensed
    milk
scant ¼ cup butter, melted
¼ tsp vanilla extract

The warm, sweet notes of the vanilla will create wondrous aromas in your kitchen while you're making these super-sweet and chewy caramels. If you want another variation, then peppermint extract works well.

1 Grease an 8-inch square cake pan, and fill the sink or a large bowl with cold water.

2 Put the sugar and milk in a large heavy-bottom pan and heat gently until the sugar has dissolved. Wash down the sides of the pan with a pastry brush dipped in water to dissolve any sugar crystals.

3 Add the corn syrup and bring to a boil. Boil steadily without stirring until a candy thermometer reaches 250°F (the firm ball stage). If you don't have a thermometer, drop a teaspoon of the mixture into a bowl of cold water. It should form a firm ball between your fingers.

4 Slowly pour in the condensed milk, butter, and vanilla extract and stir to combine. Continue boiling to 255°F (the hard ball stage). Immediately dip the base of the pan into the cold water, then pour the caramel mixture into the prepared pan. Leave to set for a short time before marking into fingers, squares, or bars; I like to use fingers.

5 Turn out the caramels when completely cold and, using oiled scissors, cut into 2½-inch x ½-inch fingers, then wrap in cellophane. These caramels keep for up to a month in a cool place.

PEANUT BRITTLE

Whether you like to snap a sweet nutty piece onto ice cream or just nibble on some when you feel the need, this brittle also makes a perfect foodie gift. Don't feel wedded to peanuts, though; toasted almonds, macadamias, or pistachios are all admirable substitutes.

PREPARATION: *15 minutes,*
  plus cooling
COOKING: *20 minutes*
MAKES: *about 1lb 6oz*

⅓ cup unsalted butter, plus extra
  for greasing
2⅔ cups salted roasted peanuts
scant 2 cups granulated sugar
¾ cup light brown sugar
½ cup corn syrup
scant ⅔ cup water

1 Liberally grease a cookie sheet or a marble slab measuring around 12 inches x 16 inches. Preheat the oven to 250°F.
2 Sprinkle the nuts on to a cookie sheet and keep warm in the oven.
3 Put the butter, sugars, and corn syrup into a large deep pan along with the water. Gently heat until the sugar has dissolved. Wash down the sides of the pan with a pastry brush dipped in water to dissolve any sugar crystals.
4 When the sugar is completely dissolved, bring to a boil. Boil steadily without stirring until a candy thermometer reaches 300°F (the hard crack stage). If you don't have a thermometer, drop a teaspoon of the mixture into a bowl of cold water and it should snap easily.
5 Quickly and thoroughly stir in the warmed nuts. Pour the mixture onto the greased cookie sheet or slab and spread out thinly. Leave to cool completely, then break into pieces. This brittle keeps for up to two weeks in an airtight container or sealed plastic bag.

PEANUT BUTTER FUDGE

PREPARATION: *20 minutes,*
 plus standing
COOKING: *10 minutes*
MAKES: *about 1lb 12¼oz*

2¼ cups granulated sugar
1 tbsp glucose syrup
scant ⅔ cup whole milk
⅔ cup unsalted butter
scant ½ cup crunchy peanut
 butter

If you like your candies with a savory edge, then this fudge is for you.
I use a crunchy peanut butter to give it an interesting texture, but use
a smooth version if you prefer your fudge silky smooth.

1 Line a 5-inch x 9-inch baking pan or dish with plastic wrap so that it
overlaps the edges. Fill a large bowl or the sink with cold water.
2 Put all the ingredients in a heavy-bottom pan and heat very gently
until the sugar has completely dissolved—take your time and ensure all
the grains are melted, otherwise the fudge won't be smooth. Use a wet
pastry brush to wash down the sides of the pan to dissolve any stray
crystals that may cause the sugar syrup to crystallize while cooking.
3 Bring to a boil and continue bubbling, stirring occasionally to ensure
the mixture isn't catching on the base, until it reaches 241°F (the soft
ball stage) on a candy thermometer. If you don't have a thermometer,
drop a teaspoon of the mixture into a bowl of cold water. Bring it
together with your fingers—it should form a soft ball.
4 Immediately plunge the base of the pan into the cold water to stop
the fudge cooking. Transfer the pan to a cold surface and leave to stand
for 5 minutes—it's important to do this; otherwise the fudge's texture
will become crumbly rather than smooth.
5 Beat the fudge mixture with an electric mixer for 5 to 10 minutes until
thick, then quickly tip into the prepared pan and smooth the surface.
6 When completely cold, cut into squares or bars. This fudge keeps for
up to a month in an airtight container or sealed plastic bag.

COFFEE AND CARDAMOM FUDGE

PREPARATION: *20 minutes, plus standing*
COOKING: *30 minutes*
MAKES: *about 35 pieces*

unsalted butter, for greasing
scant 3¼ cups granulated sugar
¾ cup water
14oz canned sweetened condensed milk
1 stick salted butter
2 tsp instant coffee powder mixed with 1 tbsp hot water
1 tsp cardamom seeds, ground

I've paired cardamom with this crumbly coffee fudge to balance the taste, and the fantastically aromatic cardamom is just heavenly.

1 Grease a 5-inch x 9-inch nonstick pan. Fill the sink or a large bowl with cold water.
2 Put all of the ingredients (discard the cardamom pods) in a heavy-bottom pan and heat very gently until the sugar has completely dissolved—take your time and ensure all the grains are melted otherwise the fudge won't be smooth. I use a wet pastry brush to wash down the sides of the pan to dissolve any stray sugar crystals that may cause the sugar syrup to crystallize while cooking.
3 Raise the heat and steadily boil the syrup to 241°F (the soft ball stage) on a candy thermometer. If you don't have a thermometer, drop a teaspoon of the mixture into a bowl of cold water. Bring it together with your fingers—it should form a soft ball. Take the pan straight off the heat and dip the base in cold water.
4 Let the sugar syrup rest for a minute or two, then with a wooden spoon, stir in the cardamom seeds. Continue stirring until the fudge starts to grain and stiffen (you will feel the consistency change against your wooden spoon), then pour into the prepared pan.
5 While still warm, mark into squares, then cut into pieces when completely cold. This fudge keeps for up to a month when stored in an airtight container, separated by layers of parchment paper.

SESAME SNAPS

PREPARATION: *5 minutes*
COOKING: *25 to 30 minutes*
MAKES: *about 1lb 3½oz*

sunflower oil, for greasing
1¾ cups sesame seeds
1¾ cups granulated sugar
1 tbsp corn syrup
scant ½ cup water

For easy packaging, I've made my sesame snaps in small pieces but you could just crack the big sheet into shards for more dramatic packages. I like the size of sesame seeds, but I've found it works well with sunflower seeds, too.

1 Grease a marble slab or heavy cookie sheet with oil, and fill the sink or a large bowl with cold water.

2 Put a large skillet over medium-low heat and dry roast the sesame seeds until lightly golden and nutty smelling—watch them like a hawk to make sure they don't burn. Keep warm.

3 Put the sugar and water into a small heavy-bottom pan and heat gently until the sugar has dissolved. Wash down the sides of the pan with a pastry brush dipped in water to dissolve any sugar crystals.

4 Boil steadily without stirring until a candy thermometer reaches 300°F (the hard crack stage—it will have a yellowish tinge). If you don't have a thermometer, drop a teaspoon of the mixture into a bowl of cold water. It should snap easily between your fingers. Then, plunge the base of the pan into the cold water.

5 Quickly mix in the sesame seeds and pour onto the prepared surface. When cold, snap into pieces. These snaps keep for up to a month among layers of waxed paper in an airtight container or sealed plastic bag.

FRUIT SALAMI

PREPARATION: *40 minutes,*
 plus maturing
COOKING: *5 to 10 minutes*
MAKES: *about 1lb 13oz, one*
 salami

1½ cups dried apricots, chopped
1½ cups dried figs, chopped
2 tbsp apricot brandy (or regular
 brandy)
1 cup walnuts, toasted and
 finely chopped
1⅓ cups candied peel
rice paper, for wrapping

A sweet "salami"—or *salame dolce*—is a speciality of southern Italy. It looks like a salami but tastes like fruity heaven. I like to serve this delicious "salami" in slices with coffee or a dessert wine or as part of a cheeseboard. *Delizioso*, as the Italians like to say.

1 Preheat the oven to 325°F. Meanwhile, whiz the apricots and figs in a food processor to make a sticky paste. Mix in the brandy and transfer the mixture to a bowl.
2 Toast the walnuts on a cookie sheet for 5 to 10 minutes. Remove from the oven, allow to cool, and chop finely. Mix in the peel and walnuts.
3 Put a large piece of parchment paper on a counter. Transfer the mixture to the parchment and, using the paper, shape the mixture into a "sausage" about 12 inches long and 2½ inches thick.
4 Next, put a piece of rice paper on a counter and put the "sausage" on one long end. Roll up tightly and trim any excess. Roll in parchment paper and twist the ends. Store in a cool place for a month before eating.

CANDY APPLES

PREPARATION: *30 minutes*
COOKING: *15 minutes*
MAKES: 12

12 small dessert apples, de-stalked
12 short bamboo skewers
sunflower oil, for greasing
2½ cups light brown sugar
½ cup cold water
1 tsp white wine vinegar
5 tbsp corn syrup

What could be a better treat for Halloween party bags than a super-sweet, crunchy candy apple? They're hard to beat.

1 Put the apples in a large bowl and briefly cover with boiling water to remove their wax coating. It will also help the sugar syrup to stick to the fruit. Drain and dry thoroughly with paper towels. Push a bamboo skewer through the base of each apple into the core and set aside.

2 Oil a large baking sheet and place on the counter as near to the stovetop as possible. Fill the sink with cold water.

3 Put the sugar in a large pan with the water. Gently heat until the sugar has dissolved. Wash down the sides of the pan with a pastry brush dipped in water to dissolve any sugar crystals.

4 When the sugar has completely dissolved, add the vinegar and corn syrup and bring to a boil. Boil steadily without stirring until a candy thermometer reaches 284°C (the soft crack stage). If you don't have a thermometer, drop a teaspoon of the mixture into a bowl of cold water. Bring it together with your fingers—it should form firm but pliable threads. When it reaches the correct temperature, plunge the base of the pan into the cold water to stop the candy cooking.

5 Dip the apples into the candy, tilting the pan and twisting the stick so that they are completely covered. Hold each apple over the pan for a few seconds to allow the excess candy to drip off. Put each apple on the parchment paper to set. Do not touch until the candy coating is completely cold. Wrap each candy apple in cellophane and store in a cool, dry place (not the refrigerator) and eat within five days.

ROSE CREAMS

PREPARATION: *25 minutes,*
  plus drying
MAKES: *20 to 22*

1¾ cups confectioners' sugar,
  sifted
2 tsp rose water
finely grated zest and juice of
  ½ lemon
pink food coloring paste

These delicate pink, scented
creams make the most of that
most old-fashioned of tastes—
rose. This recipe also works
well with rosehip syrup if you
can source that; if so, use
4 teaspoons of the syrup in
place of the rose water.

1 Put the confectioners' sugar in a bowl. Add the rose water, lemon
zest, and enough juice to make a stiff paste, then add enough pink food
coloring to delicately tint the paste.
2 Dust the counter with confectioners' sugar and knead until smooth
and evenly colored. Roll out to a ¼-inch thicknesss. Using a 1½-inch
round cutter, stamp out circles, re-rolling any trimmings. Leave the
discs to dry on a sheet of parchment paper for one to three days until
dry to the touch (this will depend on the weather!).
3 Pop into petit-four paper cups. These creams keep for up to four
weeks in an airtight container or sealed plastic bag.

For the pantry

STEM GINGER IN SYRUP

Choose smooth, plump-looking ginger for the best flavor. It will also be less fibrous.

PREPARATION: *25 minutes*
COOKING: *1 hour*
MAKES: *about 1lb 12¼oz*

5 cups ginger root
5 cups granulated sugar
1 tbsp corn syrup
4 cups water

1 The easiest way to peel the ginger is to use the edge of a teaspoon to scrape away the skin—it will enable you to get into the knobbly corners better than any vegetable peeler.
2 Cut the peeled ginger into roughly equal-sized cubes. Put into a pan and cover with cold water. Bring to a boil, then simmer for 10 minutes. Drain, re-cover with water, bring to a boil, and simmer again for 10 minutes. Drain and set aside.
3 In another pan, heat the sugar and corn syrup with the water. Heat gently to dissolve the sugar, brushing the sides of the pan with a wet pastry brush.
4 Add the ginger and boil steadily without stirring until a candy thermometer reaches 226°F (the thread stage); this should take about 30 minutes. Alternatively, if you don't have a thermometer, take a teaspoon of the mixture and hold the spoon sideways over a saucer. It should drip as a thin thread.
5 Put the ginger and syrup into sterilized jars, seal, and label. This preserve keeps indefinitely.

FLAVORED SALTS

FOR THE MIDDLE EASTERN SALT:

½ cup sea salt

1 tsp smoked paprika

1 tsp crushed red pepper flakes

2 tsp cumin seeds, lightly roasted in a dry pan

FOR THE SCANDINAVIAN SALT:

½ cup sea salt

1½ tsp dried dill

12 juniper berries, crushed and roughly chopped

FOR THE MEDITERRANEAN SALT:

½ cup sea salt

1½ tsp dried oregano

finely grated zest of 2 lemons

A salt with infused flavors can raise a humble dish to the realms of a princely one, whether added at the end of cooking or right at the beginning. The ones here are my favorites, but once you've made these why not experiment with other flavors? It's important to use a good-quality sea salt for this recipe—standard table salt may be cheaper but it won't taste half as good.

1 Put each set of ingredients into a separate bowl and stir together thoroughly.

2 Decant into jars, seal, label, and attach a wooden salt spoon to each.

CRANBERRY, ORANGE, AND GINGER CHUTNEY

PREPARATION: *20 minutes,*
 plus maturing
COOKING: *35 minutes*
MAKES: *about 2½lb*

2-inch piece ginger root, sliced
1 small cinnamon stick, broken
3 whole cloves
5 cups fresh cranberries
5 cups Bramley apples or other
 tart cooking apples, peeled,
 cored, and chopped
1 cup dried cranberries
finely grated zest and juice of
 1 orange
1⅓ cups granulated sugar
1⅔ cups white wine vinegar

Of course, this chutney is the perfect traditional accompaniment to roast turkey but it also tastes great with Swedish-style meatballs or slices of cold ham. I also stir it into a venison casserole at the end of cooking to add a fruity note.

1 Cut out a 4½-inch square of cheesecloth and put the ginger and spices in the center. Bring together the corners and tie firmly with a piece of kitchen string.

2 Put the cheesecloth bag and the remaining ingredients into a large pan or a preserving pan. Heat gently until all the sugar has dissolved.

3 Bring to a boil, then lower the heat to a simmer and cook for 30 minutes until thickened. To tell if the chutney is ready, draw a wooden spoon across the base of the pan—it should leave a visible channel for 1 to 2 seconds.

4 While the chutney is still hot, decant into hot, sterilized jars, cover with a disc of waxed paper, and seal with vinegar-proof lids.

5 Label when cold and leave to mature in a cool, dark place for a month before eating. This chutney keeps for up to a year unopened. Once it's opened, refrigerate and use within four weeks.

Add its many uses to the label so the recipient of your gift can enjoy it whenever they like.

THAI GREEN CURRY PASTE

PREPARATION: *25 minutes*
COOKING: *2 minutes*
MAKES: *about 11¼oz*

1 tsp cumin seeds
2 tsp coriander seeds
6 large green chiles, roughly
   chopped, including seeds
2 shallots, roughly chopped
2-inch piece galangal or ginger
   root, peeled and chopped
3 garlic cloves, crushed
2 stalks lemongrass, trimmed
   and chopped
1 cup fresh cilantro, leaves and
   stalks, roughly chopped
finely grated zest and juice of
   2 limes
3 tbsp sunflower oil
2 tsp fish sauce

This aromatic and vibrant curry paste is simple to make and really packs a punch in the flavor stakes. What's more, it's totally adaptable and can make the base of any curry you happen to like—meat, fish, or vegetable.

1 Put a small pan over medium heat and dry roast the cumin and coriander seeds for a minute or so until lightly toasted and aromatic—don't leave the pan unattended for even a moment as they burn easily. Allow to cool for a few minutes.
2 Put all of the remaining ingredients into a food processor with the cooled seeds and whiz to a coarse purée—but make sure that all the ingredients, particularly the fibrous lemongrass, are properly processed.
3 Divide the paste among sterilized jars, seal, and label. This paste keeps for two weeks in the fridge.

HARISSA PASTE

PREPARATION: *20 minutes,
    plus soaking*
COOKING: **5 minutes**
MAKES: *about 2½oz*

Harissa is a wonderfully versatile paste—it's spicy and fragrant—and can transform stews or soups, can be used as a rub for meat or poultry, or simply stirred into yogurt or couscous. It's powerful, though, so package in small spice jars, as a little goes a long way.

3 cups dried whole red chiles
1 tsp caraway seeds
½ tsp cumin seeds
1 tsp coriander seeds
2 garlic cloves, roughly chopped
juice of ¼ lemon
½ tsp salt
3–4 tbsp olive oil, plus extra
    for covering

1 Put the chiles into a bowl and cover with boiling water. Let soak for an hour.
2 Dry roast the whole spices in a small skillet over medium heat for a few minutes until toasted and they smell aromatic. Keep a close watch on them so that they don't burn.
3 Drain the chiles, discarding the water. Put into a food processor with the toasted spices, garlic, lemon juice, and salt, and blend to a paste.
4 Blend in enough of the oil to loosen the mixture slightly. Transfer to sterilized jars, leaving a small gap at the top. Cover with a thin layer of oil. Seal and label. This paste keeps for up to four months.

SPICY LIME PICKLE

PREPARATION: *25 minutes,
    plus maturing*
COOKING: **5 minutes**
MAKES: *about 4lb*

Move over mango chutney, it's time to try and savor this spicy pickle. This classic Indian accompaniment often gets overlooked, but once you've tried it—the limes are so flavorsome—you'll be making batches to persuade everyone to fly the flag for this delicious Indian preserve.

2 cups white wine vinegar
1¾ cups granulated sugar
juice of 2 limes
12 limes, each cut into 6 wedges
2¼ tbsp salt
5 whole dried chiles
1-inch piece ginger root, sliced

1 Put the vinegar and sugar into a large pan. Heat gently until the sugar has dissolved. Add the lime juice and boil for 2 minutes. Let cool for 10 minutes.
2 Pack the limes tightly into hot, sterilized jars, layering with salt, chiles, and ginger as you do so.
3 Pour the vinegar mixture into the jars, making sure the limes are completely covered. To stop them bobbing above the surface of the liquid, tuck a wedge of folded parchment paper on the top. Seal and leave in a cool, dark place for six weeks before eating.

SWEET AND SPICY MANGO CHUTNEY

PREPARATION: *35 minutes*
COOKING: *35 minutes*
MAKES: *about 1lb 2oz*

½ tsp cumin seeds
½ tsp crushed red pepper flakes
1 cup cider vinegar
1 cup light brown sugar
2¼lb ripe mangoes (4 to 5
  mangoes, depending on size),
  peeled, pitted, and chopped
1 tsp nigella seeds

I use Alphonso mangoes to make this chutney. They only have a short season but are deeply aromatic and have an intense peachy, honeyed flavor. It doesn't matter if you can't find this variety, though, as the chutney will still be delicious. I have tried making this chutney in larger batches but the cooking time has to increase and I find it loses its freshness—but if you don't mind that, then feel free to double or triple the recipe quantities below.

1 Put a small pan over medium heat. Dry-roast the cumin seeds for 30 seconds to 1 minute, shaking the pan often. Be careful not to burn them and don't leave them unattended.
2 Put the cumin seeds and the remaining ingredients, except for the nigella seeds, into a preserving pan or large deep pan and set over low heat until the sugar has dissolved.
3 Bring to a boil, then lower the heat to a simmer, and cook for 30 minutes until thickened. To tell if the chutney is ready, draw a wooden spoon across the base of the pan—it should leave a visible channel for 1 to 2 seconds. Now, stir in the nigella seeds.
4 While the chutney is still hot, decant into hot, sterilized jars, cover with discs of waxed paper, and seal with vinegar-proof lids. Label when cold. You can enjoy this chutney the next day, but it will keep for up to a year unopened. Refrigerate after opening and use within four weeks.

Preserving jars come in a wonderful array of clipdown tops for perfect preserves every time.

RIGHT *(clockwise from front left) Thai green curry paste; Spicy lime pickle; Sweet and spicy mango chutney; and Cranberry, orange, and ginger chutney.* **LEFT** *Harissa paste.*

A homemade mustard really packs a great punch. Here you can try just one or all three for slightly different flavor combinations. I source large packs of mustard seeds from ethnic food stores.

FOR THE CHILE AND GARLIC MUSTARD:

generous ½ cup black mustard seeds

¼ cup yellow mustard seeds

½ cup white wine vinegar

2 tsp crushed red pepper flakes

2 tsp paprika

3 garlic cloves, crushed

1 tsp salt

A TRIO OF MUSTARDS

PREPARATION: *30 minutes,*
  plus standing
MAKES: *about 10½oz of each*
  mustard

**FOR THE WHOLEGRAIN HONEY
MUSTARD:**
generous ½ cup black mustard
  seeds
¼ cup yellow mustard seeds
½ cup white wine vinegar
2 tbsp liquid honey
1 tsp salt

FOR THE TARRAGON MUSTARD:
¼ cup black mustard seeds
generous ½ cup yellow mustard
  seeds
½ cup cider vinegar
1 shallot, finely chopped
1 tbsp tarragon leaves, chopped
1 tsp salt

1 Whichever mustard you want to make, they all start off in the same way. Put the mustard seeds in a non-metallic bowl, pour in the vinegar, cover, and let stand for 24 hours at room temperature.

2 Stir the rest of the flavorings into each bowl, for whichever you're making. Add a drop more vinegar if the mixture seems too dry. Now, you can leave the seeds whole as they are in the mustard or put the mixture into a food processor and blend for a minute or two to break some of them down. I prefer to do the latter as it makes a creamier mustard.

3 Whichever method you choose, decant the mustards into small jars, seal with vinegar-proof lids, and let mature for at least two weeks to allow the flavors to mingle. These mustards keep for up to a year unopened. Once opened, use within two months.

From the garden

Make a personalized and hand-stamped label and simply clip onto some string with a mini peg.

THIS PAGE *(clockwise from top) Spicy piccalilli; Spicy barbecue sauce; and Pumpkin relish.*

SPICY PICCALILLI

PREPARATION: *30 minutes,*
 plus salting
COOKING: *25 minutes*
MAKES: *about 4½lb*

5½lb mixed vegetables, such as
 cauliflower, French beans, green
 beans, shallots
cooking salt
¼ cup cornstarch
6 cups distilled white vinegar
1 tbsp ground turmeric
1 tbsp dry English mustard
1 tbsp ground ginger
⅔ cup granulated sugar
½ tsp crushed red pepper flakes

Piccalilli is the English version of spiced Indian vegetables and is a great way of using up a glut of summer vegetables. Enjoy with a wedge of pork pie, cold meats, or tangy cheeses for a simple lunch.

1 Cut the vegetables into bite-sized pieces. Put in a colander, layering with plenty of salt as you go (sit the colander on the draining board or on a plate to collect the juices). Put a plate on top and weigh it down with heavy pans. Let stand for 24 hours.
2 Quickly rinse the salt off the vegetables under running water and pat dry with paper towels.
3 Mix the cornstarch with 2 tablespoons of the vinegar and set aside.
4 Put the remaining ingredients in a large pan. Stir together then add the vegetables. Bring to a boil, then simmer for 5 to 10 minutes until the vegetables are only just tender—keep checking with the point of a knife as they mustn't overcook and should still have some crunch to them.
5 Using a slotted spoon, remove the vegetables and pack into hot, sterilized jars. Stir the cornstarch mixture into the cooking liquid. Bring to a boil and simmer for 3 to 5 minutes, stirring, until slightly thickened.
6 Pour the vinegar mixture over the vegetables and seal with vinegar-proof lids. Store in a cool, dark place for a month before eating. This keeps for up to a year unopened. Once opened, eat within a month.

BARBECUE SAUCE

PREPARATION: *10 minutes*
COOKING: *30 to 35 minutes*
MAKES: *about 1¾ cups*

2 tbsp sunflower oil
1 medium onion, finely chopped
scant ⅔ cup tomato ketchup
1 tsp cayenne pepper
3 tbsp Worcestershire sauce
scant ⅔ cup cider vinegar
2 tbsp clear honey
1 tsp Dijon mustard
1 star anise

This wonderfully versatile sauce can be used as a condiment itself or brushed onto meat and poultry during cooking to add tangy spicy notes.

1 Heat the sunflower oil in a pan and gently fry the onion for 20 minutes until soft.
2 Add the remaining ingredients, bring to a boil, and then simmer for 5 minutes. Cool slightly.
3 Remove the star anise and discard. Blend in a food processor or blender until very smooth. Pour into sterilized bottles and seal, then label. This spicy sauce keeps for up to two months. Refrigerate after opening and use within four weeks. Shake before use.

PUMPKIN RELISH

PREPARATION: *20 minutes*
COOKING: *1 hour*
MAKES: *about 1lb 12¼oz*

9 cups pumpkin or butternut
  squash, peeled, deseeded, and
  diced
1 large onion, chopped
¾ cup soft dark brown sugar
1 tsp celery seeds
1 tsp fennel seeds
1½ cups cider vinegar

Take full advantage of the bumper bounty of pumpkins and squash in the fall to make this delicious relish. I like to serve it simply, with some good cheese and bread.

1 Put all of the ingredients into a large deep pan or a preserving pan and set over low heat until the sugar has dissolved.
2 Bring to a boil, then lower the heat to a simmer, and cook for around 45 to 60 minutes until the pumpkin is tender but not disintegrated.
3 While the relish is still hot, decant into hot, sterilized jars, cover with discs of waxed paper (the waxy side should be relish side down), and seal with vinegar-proof lids. Label when cold. Store in a cool, dry place for a month before eating. This relish keeps for up to a year unopened. Refrigerate after opening and use within four weeks.

GOOSEBERRY CHUTNEY

PREPARATION: *25 minutes*
COOKING: *1 hour 30 minutes*
MAKES: *about 2lb 14oz*

3 slices *ginger root*
1 tsp *coriander seeds*
6 *black peppercorns*
9 cups *cooking gooseberries,*
  cleaned
2 cups *raisins*
1½ cups *red onions, finely*
  chopped
generous 1 cup *light brown*
  sugar
2½ cups *white wine vinegar*

One of my favorite lunches is homemade bread, a tangy cheese, and a dollop of my gooseberry chutney. I think it would make a great gift for any foodie. If gooseberries are scarce, green tomatoes work well too.

1 Lay out a 4½-inch square of cheesecloth on a counter and put the ginger and spices in the center. Draw the corners together and fasten with some kitchen string.

2 Put the remaining ingredients and the spice bag into a large deep pan or preserving pan and set over low heat until the sugar has dissolved.

3 Bring to a boil, then lower the heat to a simmer, and cook for 1 hour to 1 hour 30 minutes until thickened. To tell if the chutney is ready, draw a wooden spoon across the base of the pan—it should leave a visible channel for 1 to 2 seconds. Remove and discard the spice bag.

4 While the chutney is still hot, decant into hot, sterilized jars, cover with discs of waxed paper (the waxy side should be chutney side down), and seal with vinegar-proof lids. Label when cold. Store in a cool, dry place for a month before eating. This chutney keeps for up to a year unopened. Refrigerate after opening and use within four weeks.

Tying on a vintage spoon means the gift can be enjoyed as soon as it's unwrapped.

RIGHT *(from left to right) Gooseberry chutney; Fig relish; and Sweet chile sauce.*

SWEET CHILE SAUCE

PREPARATION: *15 minutes*
COOKING: *30 minutes*
MAKES: *2⅔ cups*

2¼ cups granulated sugar
2½ cups water
6 large red chile peppers
1 tbsp crushed red pepper flakes
scant ⅔ cup rice vinegar
3 garlic cloves, crushed
1 tbsp fish sauce
2 tbsp cornstarch

Here's one for all lovers of Thai flavors. The enduring partnership of sweet and spicy is a winner and I like to use this fiery and delicous sauce as a marinade or as a dipping sauce for Thai fish cakes.

1 Put the sugar into a large pan with the water and heat gently until the sugar has dissolved completely.
2 Add the remaining ingredients, except the cornstarch, and bring to a boil. Lower the heat to a simmer and bubble for about 30 minutes until the sauce is lightly syrupy.
3 Put the cornstarch into a small bowl and stir in a spoonful or two of the chile sauce to blend into a paste. Tip back into the pan and bring to a boil, stirring constantly. Cook for 1 to 2 minutes.
4 Using a sterilized funnel, pour into sterilized bottles, seal, and then label when cold. This sauce keeps for up to a year. Once opened, store it in the refrigerator and use within three months. Shake before use.

FIG RELISH

PREPARATION: *40 minutes*
COOKING: *1 hour*
MAKES: *about 1lb 14¾oz*

1 tbsp sunflower oil
1½ cups onions, finely chopped
4 black peppercorns
1 star anise
2½ cups fresh figs, chopped
2 cups Bramley apples or
  other tart cooking apples,
  peeled and cored
finely grated zest and juice of
  1 orange
generous 1 cup soft dark brown
  sugar
generous ¾ cup cider vinegar
½ tsp salt

As this relish has a shorter cooking time, it doesn't keep for as long. It's marvelous with a crumbly feta cheese or extra-old Cheddar.

1 In a large deep pan, heat the oil and gently fry the onions for 10 minutes until softened.
2 Lay out a 4½-inch square of cheesecloth on a counter and put the spices in the center. Draw the corners together and fasten with string.
3 Put the remaining ingredients, along with the spice bag, into the pan and set over low heat until the sugar has dissolved.
4 Bring to a boil, then lower the heat to a simmer and cook for 35 to 40 minutes until thickened. To tell if the chutney is ready, draw a wooden spoon across the base of the pan—it should leave a visible channel for 1 to 2 seconds. When it's ready, discard the spice bag.
5 While the chutney is still hot, decant into hot, sterilized jars, cover with a disc of waxed paper, and seal with vinegar-proof lids then label when cold. Store in a cool, dry place for a month before eating. This relish keeps for up to six months unopened but once opened it should be refrigerated and used within four weeks.

ASIAN-SPICED VEGETABLES

A riot of color in a jar is the first you see of these preserved vegetables, but their taste packs a punch, too. This is an impressive gift for anyone who loves food from the East.

1 Slice the vegetables finely with a mandolin or sharp knife. Pack into sterilized jars in layers.

2 Put the vinegar in a pan along with the ginger, pepper, pepper flakes, and the water. Bring to a boil then pour over the vegetables, making sure they are fully covered.

3 Seal with vinegar-proof lids and label. Store in a cool, dark place for one month before using. These spiced vegetables keep for six months.

PICKLED ONIONS

PREPARATION: *60 minutes,*
  plus soaking and maturing
COOKING: *2 minutes*
MAKES: *about 3lb 15oz*

4 cups distilled vinegar
1 tsp fennel seeds
1 tsp celery seeds
1 tsp black peppercorns
4 bay leaves
1 tsp yellow mustard seeds
1 tsp blade mace
¼ cup cooking salt
2½ cups boiling water
1lb 11¾oz pickling onions,
  peeled and left whole

All that is needed to accompany these feisty crunchy pickles for a delicious dinner is a crusty loaf, strong cheese, and a good cider.

1 Put all of the ingredients, except the salt, boiling water, and onions, into a stainless steel pan. Cover and heat gently until just under boiling point. Remove from the heat and let infuse overnight.

2 Put the salt into a large non-metallic bowl and cover with the measured boiling water. Stir to dissolve and leave this brine to cool.

3 Cover the onions with boiling water. Let stand for a couple of minutes, then drain and peel.

4 Add the onions to the brine, cover, and leave for two days.

5 Drain the onions, rinse, and pack tightly into sterilized jars. Drain the pickling vinegar, discarding the spices and pour over the onions, covering them completely. Seal and label. Leave for at least three months before eating. These onions keep for up to a year unopened. Once opened, use within two months.

PREPARATION: *20 minutes,
  plus sitting*
MAKES: 4lb

2 red peppers
3 carrots
1 red onion
1 Daikon radish
¼ white cabbage

3¾ cups Japanese rice vinegar
1-inch piece ginger root, peeled
  and sliced
1 tbsp Sichuan peppers
1 tsp crushed red pepper flakes
2 cups water

ENGLISH PLUM CHEESE

PREPARATION: *30 minutes*
COOKING: *1 hour 5 minutes*
MAKES: *about 1lb 12¼oz*

2¼lb plums, quartered
granulated sugar

Fruit cheese is so called as
it slices just like cheese. It's
popular "across the pond" and
works particularly well as an
accompaniment to duck and
game or with a wedge of mature
Cheddar, the kind that tickles
the roof of your mouth.

1 Put the plums into a large deep pan and cover with water—there's
no need to peel or pit them. Bring to a boil, then simmer for
20 minutes until the fruit is very soft. Skim away any of the skin or pits
that rise to the surface.

2 Push the plums and the juices through a sieve, getting as much purée
as you can. Measure the purée and allow 1⅔ cups of sugar for every
2½ cups of purée you obtain.

3 Put the purée and sugar into a nonstick pan and heat slowly to
dissolve the sugar. Turn up the heat and boil for about 45 minutes until
the mixture is thick—a wooden spoon drawn across the bottom of the
pan should leave a clean line.

4 Transfer the cheese into a lightly oiled square or rectangular mold
(I find that disposable foil containers work well, too). Alternatively, use
small jars or dishes and cover with a disc of waxed paper. Cover the
containers or seal the jars and leave the cheese for two months before
eating. Wrap in waxed paper and decorate to give as a gift. This cheese
keeps for up to a year unopened. Once opened, use within two months.

PREPARATION: *30 minutes*
COOKING: *1 hour 10 minutes*
MAKES: *about 2¼lb*

5½lb quince
5 whole cloves
8 cups water
granulated sugar

Despite looking like a cross
between an apple and a pear, a
quince straight from the bush
is inedible. A short cooking
journey transforms this fruit
into a delightful pink jelly that's
delicious with duck and game
or with cheese. A spoonful of
this jelly stirred into gravies and
savory sauces adds a pleasing
depth of flavor, too.

QUINCE JELLY

1 Roughly chop the quince into 1¼-inch chunks—there's no need to
peel or core them, everything goes into the pan.
2 Put the fruit into a preserving pan with the cloves and the water. Bring
to a boil then simmer for about 1 hour until very soft and pulpy.
3 Carefully pour the quince and the liquid into a jelly bag and let strain
overnight—do not be tempted to extract more juice by pushing down
the mixture as it will make the jelly cloudy.
4 Measure the liquid: for every 2½ cups you will need 2 cups of sugar.
Put the juice and sugar into a preserving pan and heat gently to dissolve
the sugar. Bring to a boil and boil for 5 to 10 minutes until setting point
is reached, but I'd check after 5 minutes. To test, put a teaspoon of jelly
onto a cold saucer, leave it to cool for a few minutes, then push it with
your finger. If it's reached setting point, it should wrinkle. If not, continue
boiling and testing until setting point is reached.
5 Skim any scum from the surface with a slotted spoon and transfer the
jelly into hot, sterilized jars and seal. Label when cold. This jelly keeps
for up to a year unopened. Once opened, use within three months.

RED ONION MARMALADE

PREPARATION: *25 minutes*
COOKING: *1 hour 30 minutes*
MAKES: *about 1lb 4oz*

2 tbsp olive oil
9 cups red onions, finely sliced
1 tsp salt
¾ cup plus 1 tbsp soft light
  brown sugar
scant ⅔ cup red wine
1 tbsp sherry vinegar
1 tbsp redcurrant jelly

I wouldn't be without a jar of this magical marmalade in my cupboard. It has myriad uses, from livening up a sandwich, enhancing a casserole, or just smothering over sausages.

1 Heat the oil in a wide skillet and add the onions along with the salt. Cover the onions with a circle of dampened parchment paper and a tightly fitting lid. Cook on the lowest heat for around 1 hour, stirring occasionally, until the onions are meltingly tender.
2 Discard the paper, turn up the heat, and stir in the sugar. Cook, stirring often, until the liquid has evaporated and the onions are a deep brown color (but not burned).
3 Pour in the wine and bubble until the liquid has evaporated, then stir in the redcurrant jelly and check the seasoning.
4 Divide among sterilized jars while still hot, seal, and then label when cold. This condiment keeps for up to a year unopened. Once opened, store it in the refrigerator and use within six weeks.

Create a beautiful box of goodies to accompany this savory marmalade.

SUNBLUSH TOMATOES

PREPARATION: **15 minutes, plus draining**
COOKING: **8 to 10 hours**
MAKES: *about 2lb*

4½lb ripe plum tomatoes
2 tsp superfine sugar
1 tbsp fresh oregano or marjoram leaves, plus extra sprigs
1 tsp salt
good-quality extra virgin olive oil, for covering

The long, slow cooking at a low temperature draws out the natural sweetness of the humble plum tomato, creating a delicious and intense flavor that you can enjoy year round.

1 Set wire racks over rimmed cookie sheets. Halve the tomatoes and arrange closely together on the racks cut side down. Let drain for 30 minutes. Meanwhile, preheat the oven to the lowest temperature setting you can—I've used 175°F.

2 Turn the tomato halves over and sprinkle with the sugar, oregano or marjoram, and salt.

3 Put the tomatoes in the oven and wedge a skewer in the door to keep it slightly ajar. Cook for 8 to 10 hours until dried out—this is a matter of preference. I prefer a softer sunblush texture and flavor while others like to dry them out completely. It's up to you.

4 Pack into sterilized jars and submerge entirely with olive oil. Add a sprig of fresh oregano or marjoram if you like, then seal. These tomatoes keep for up to a year unopened. Once opened, store in the refrigerator and use within two weeks. You can use the tomato-infused oil for dressings or cooking, too.

PICKLED CHERRIES

PREPARATION: *25 minutes,*
  plus standing
COOKING: *7 minutes*
MAKES: *about 2½lb*

2¼lb cherries (I use Morello but
  Duke or Royal varieties work
  well too)
2¼ cups granulated sugar
1⅔ cups distilled white vinegar
¾-inch piece ginger root, sliced
6 cloves
1 cinnamon stick, broken in half

Make these super-useful cherries for yourself or a friend who hankers after a sweet and sour cocktail, as a grown-up accompaniment to roast meats, especially pork and game, or to serve with cheese.

1 Prepare the cherries. Whether you pit the cherries or not is up to you; I prefer to keep them in, as the pits impart a pleasing, subtle almond flavor. I also keep the stalks intact because they look prettier on the plate. If you decide to keep the pits, pierce each cherry two or three times with a skewer.
2 Put all the remaining ingredients, except the cherries, in a deep pan and heat gently to dissolve the sugar.
3 Add the cherries to the pan, cover, and poach for about 5 to 7 minutes until just tender. Using a slotted spoon, transfer the cherries to hot sterilized jars, leaving a ½-inch gap at the top.
4 Cover the fruit with the poaching syrup, tucking the ginger and cinnamon pieces into the jars too, and seal. Leave in a cool, dark place for a month before giving away or eating.

A wonderful spread of jars.
Here we have a mixture of
Fruits of the forest preserve
and Apricot and amaretto jelly.

APRICOT AND AMARETTO JELLY

PREPARATION: *35 minutes,*
  plus standing
COOKING: *about 25 minutes*
MAKES: *about 2½lb*

2¼lb ripe apricots
4½ cups granulated sugar
juice of 1 lemon
1¼ cups water
2 tbsp amaretto

Apricots have a natural affinity with almonds. In this jelly, I enhance this by extracting the pleasing almond flavor of the apricot kernels and by adding some amaretto liqueur.

1 Halve the apricots, remove their pits and set aside. Quarter or roughly chop the apricot flesh, depending on how chunky you like your jelly.

2 Crack open the apricot pits with a pair of nutcrackers. Remove the kernels and discard the shells. Bring a pan of water to a boil, add the apricots kernels, and boil for 2 minutes. Drain.

3 Put two or three saucers in the freezer so they're ready to use to test for a set later on.

4 Put the apricots, blanched kernels, and lemon juice into a preserving pan along with the water. Simmer gently for 5 to 10 minutes until the fruit is tender—this time will depend on their ripeness.

5 Add the sugar and heat gently until dissolved—it's important to make sure all the crystals are dissolved.

6 Bring to a boil and boil for 10 to 15 minutes; stir from time to time, as this jelly can catch on the base of the pan. After 10 minutes, test for the setting point: put a teaspoon of the jelly on one of the freezing-cold saucers (take the pan off the heat while you do this). Leave for 1 to 2 minutes then push the jelly with your finger—when it's ready, it should wrinkle. If it fails to wrinkle, continue boiling and test for a set every 5 minutes. (If you're using a candy thermometer, the setting temperature is 220°F.)

7 Turn off the heat and let stand for 15 minutes. Skim off any scum, ladle the jelly into hot sterilized jars, cover the surface with discs of waxed paper (the waxy side should be jelly side down), and seal. Label the jars when completely cold. This jelly keeps for up to a year unopened. Once opened, use within two months.

FRUITS OF THE FOREST PRESERVE

PREPARATION: *15 minutes*
COOKING: *20 minutes, plus*
  macerating
MAKES: *2½lb*

2¼lb mixed summer berries,
  such as raspberries,
  blackberries, tayberries,
  loganberries, blackcurrants, or
  blueberries
4½ cups granulated sugar
generous ¾ cup water
juice of 2 lemons

Whatever berries you can get your hands on will be transformed into this beautifully colored and wonderfully tasty jelly. Make sure that your mix of fruit contains a high proportion of high-pectin berries (such as raspberries, redcurrants, and blackcurrants) to ensure a good set.

1 Two days before you plan to make the preserve, put the fruit and sugar in a large bowl, stir carefully, cover with plastic wrap, and let macerate at room temperature. The sugar will mingle with the fruit and draw out their natural juices.
2 Put two or three saucers in the freezer so they're ready to use to test for a set later on.
3 Put the berries and sugar in a preserving pan with the water and the lemon juice. Heat gently to dissolve the sugar—it's important to make sure all the crystals are melted.
4 Bring to a boil and boil for 10 to 15 minutes. After 10 minutes, test for the setting point: put a teaspoon of the jelly on one of the freezing-cold saucers (take the pan off the heat while you do this). Leave for 1 to 2 minutes then push the jelly with your finger—when it's ready, it should wrinkle. If it fails to wrinkle, continue boiling and test for a set every 5 minutes. (If you're using a candy thermometer, the setting temperature is 220°F.)
5 Turn off the heat and let stand for 15 minutes. Skim off any scum, ladle the jelly into hot sterilized jars, cover the surface with discs of waxed paper (the waxy side should be jelly side down), and seal. Label the jars when completely cold. This jelly keeps for up to a year unopened. Once opened, use within two months.

Even the simplest jar can be used and transformed with a fabric or paper top.

Capture ripe peaches in a heady syrup for a serving of summertime, whatever the time of year. These peaches taste great served with ice cream and crêpes—why not enjoy a small glass of the peach-flavored liqueur alongside?

BOURBON PEACHES

PREPARATION: *15 minutes,*
  plus standing
COOKING: *2 minutes*
MAKES: *4lb*

1 vanilla bean, split
¾ cup granulated sugar
generous 3¾ cups water
6 to 8 ripe peaches, halved
  and pitted
1¼ cups Bourbon whisky

1 Put the vanilla bean, sugar, and water into a large pan and heat gently until the sugar has dissolved. Turn up the heat and boil for 2 minutes, then set aside to cool.

2 Pierce each peach several times with a skewer. Pack into a sterilized jar.

3 Stir the Bourbon into the sugar syrup and pour over the peaches, making sure they are submerged entirely. Seal and let stand in a cool, dark place for two months before eating. These peaches keep indefinitely if unopened. Once opened, eat within one month.

STRAWBERRY PASTILLES

PREPARATION: *30 minutes*
COOKING: *30 to 45 minutes*
MAKES: *about 1lb 7oz*

1lb 2oz strawberries, hulled
*2¼ cups gelling sugar**
juice of ½ lemon
superfine sugar, for sprinkling

Take full advantage of any glut of strawberries, either from your garden or a trip to a local pick-your-own farm, and transform this summery fruit into chewy, luscious jellies, which will lengthen the time you can enjoy the wonderful taste of these delicious berries.

1 Dampen an 11-inch x 7-inch baking pan with water and then line with plastic wrap.
2 Put the strawberries in a food processor and purée until smooth.
3 Put this purée, along with the sugar and lemon juice into a nonstick pan and heat gently to dissolve the sugar. (*If you don't have gelling sugar, use the same amount of granulated sugar and add the amount of pectin suggested on the package.) Bring to a boil and cook steadily, stirring constantly until the purée is very thick—it'll take around 15 minutes. Pay close attention, as once it starts to thicken it is prone to catching on the bottom of the pan.
4 Next, pour into the prepared baking pan, spread out evenly with the back of a spoon, and let set overnight in a cool place.
5 Turn out onto a chopping board and cut into squares (I make mine around ¾-inch square or use a small heart cutter). Sprinkle plenty of superfine sugar onto a sheet of parchment paper and roll the jelly cubes in the sugar to coat. These pastilles keep for four weeks in an airtight container or sealed plastic bag.

The delights
of chocolate

MENDIANTS

PREPARATION: *20 minutes,*
  plus setting
COOKING: *5 minutes*
MAKES: *about 25*

3½oz semisweet, milk, or white
  chocolate, broken into pieces

TO DECORATE:
raisins
crystallized violets or roses
strips of dried figs
candied peel
pistachio nuts
colored sprinkles

Make these sophisticated chocolate buttons with your favorite type of chocolate—whether it's white, milk, or semisweet—or, even better, a special selection of all three types.

1 Draw 25 1½-inch circles on a large piece of silicone paper (or parchment paper) with a black marker. Turn the paper over and put on to a counter or marble slab—ideally choose somewhere you can leave the buttons to cool without moving them as they will take a couple of hours to set.

2 Put two-thirds of the chocolate into a heatproof bowl set over a pan of gently simmering water. Once the chocolate is melted and has reached 113°F, stir in the remaining chocolate. The temperature should drop and once it is at 86°F it is ready to use. This two-step melting is a simple form of tempering, which keeps the chocolate looking glossy. However, if you don't mind losing the glossiness of the chocolate, you can melt it all at once and continue the recipe.

3 Using a teaspoon, drizzle a little of the chocolate on to one of the circles and spread into a button shape. Only shape five or six at a time, keeping the rest of the chocolate over the hot water.

4 Garnish each button with your chosen decorations, then continue in batches with the rest of the chocolate. Let set completely before peeling them off the paper and packing into cellophane bags or jars. Don't chill them as the chocolate will lose its lovely glossiness.

WHITE CHOCOLATE AND ROSEMARY TRUFFLES

These rich and interesting truffles offer a delicate balance of white chocolate with aromatic rosemary. I find that the rosemary tempers the sweetness of the white chocolate so it doesn't end up too sickly. See what you think.

PREPARATION: *40 minutes*
COOKING: *5 minutes*
MAKES: *about 30*

scant ½ cup heavy cream
a large sprig rosemary
7oz white chocolate, broken into pieces
1 tbsp corn syrup
2 tbsp unsalted butter
sunflower oil, for greasing
confectioners' sugar, for dusting

1 Put the cream and rosemary in a small pan and bring to a boil—this is important, otherwise the ganache won't thicken when beaten. Put the chocolate into a heatproof bowl. Pour over the cream and rosemary and stir once or twice.

2 Set the bowl over a pan of very gently simmering water, add the corn syrup and butter. Let melt, stirring once or twice to combine. Set aside until cooled to room temperature.

3 Discard the rosemary. When cool, beat the mixture with an electric mixer until soft, fluffy, and paler in color. Pour into a lightly oiled disposable foil container (7 inches x 5 inches) and put into the refrigerator to set.

4 Lay out a large piece of parchment paper on your counter and dust liberally with confectioners' sugar.

5 Retrieve the foil container from the refrigerator and snip its edges so that you can carefully peel them away. Turn out the truffle block onto a board. Cut into 1¼-inch cubes (you'll need to clean the knife with paper towels every few cuts) and transfer the truffles to the parchment paper as you go.

6 Dust the truffle cubes with more confectioners' sugar and roll, pressing gently, to cover them completely.

7 Transfer the truffles to petit-four paper cups and arrange in lidded boxes. Store in the refrigerator, where they can last for up to two weeks.

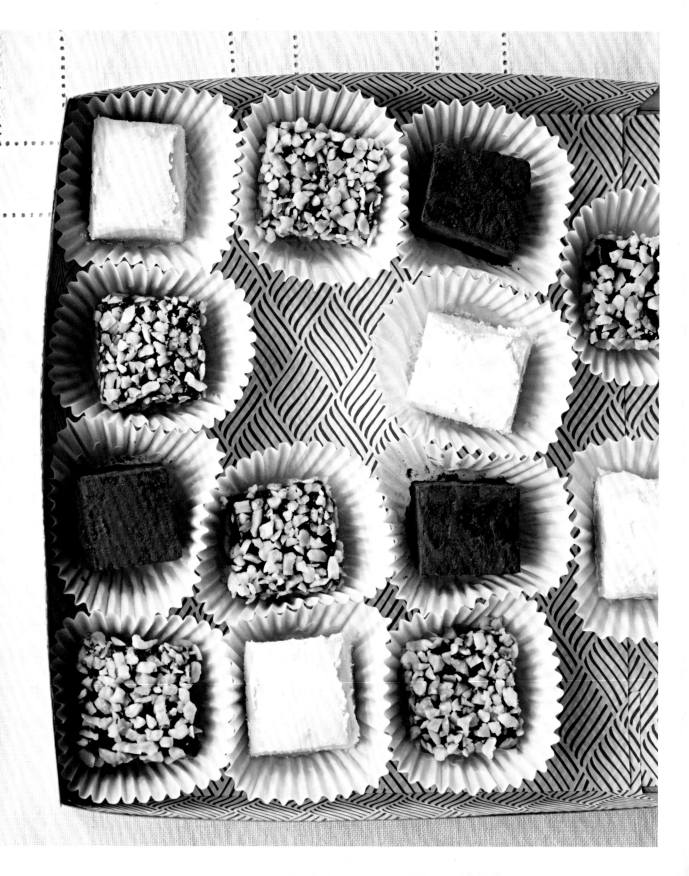

HAZELNUT TRUFFLES

PREPARATION: *40 minutes,*
 plus chilling
COOKING: *5 minutes*
MAKES: *about 35*

½ cup heavy cream
4oz milk chocolate, broken into
 pieces
½ cup chocolate hazelnut spread
1 tbsp corn syrup
3½ tbsp unsalted butter
sunflower oil, for greasing
scant 1 cup hazelnuts, toasted
 and finely chopped

I love making truffles, but my least favorite part is rolling them into balls as I tend to get covered in melted chocolate. Instead, I pour the mixture into a tray and cut them into squares once set. It's much quicker and these cubic delights look pleasingly different to the usual shapes.

1 Bring the cream to a boil in a small pan—this is important, otherwise the ganache won't thicken when beaten. Put the chocolate into a heatproof bowl. Pour over the cream and stir once or twice.

2 Set the bowl over a pan of very gently simmering water, add the spread, corn syrup, and butter. Let melt, stirring once or twice to combine. Set aside until cooled to room temperature.

3 When cool, beat the mixture with an electric mixer until soft, fluffy, and paler in color. Pour into a lightly oiled disposable foil container (7 inches x 5 inches) and put into the refrigerator to set.

4 Lay out a large piece of parchment paper on your counter and spread half of the chopped hazelnuts onto it.

5 Retrieve the foil container from the refrigerator and snip its edges so that you can carefully peel them away. Turn out the truffle block onto a board. Cut into 1¼-inch cubes (you'll need to clean the knife with paper towels every few cuts) and transfer the truffles to the nut-covered parchment paper as you go.

6 Sprinkle the remaining hazelnuts over the truffle cubes and roll, pressing gently, to cover them completely in the nuts.

7 Transfer the truffles to petit-four paper cups and arrange in lidded boxes. Store in the refrigerator, where they can last for up to two weeks.

WHISKY AND GINGER TRUFFLES

PREPARATION: **40 minutes,**
  plus chilling
COOKING: **5 minutes**
MAKES: **about 35 to 40**

scant ⅔ cup heavy cream
9oz semisweet chocolate, broken
  into pieces
3 balls stem ginger, diced, and
  1 tbsp of the syrup
1 tbsp corn syrup
3½ tbsp unsalted butter
2 tbsp whisky
sunflower oil, for greasing
unsweetened cocoa powder, for
  dusting

With a rich and intense flavor, these truffles are truly divine. This truffle mixture works well with most liqueurs, especially brandy, amaretto, and cointreau; though do omit the ginger and syrup if you're varying flavors.

1 Put the cream in a small pan and bring to a boil—this is important, otherwise the ganache won't thicken when beaten. Put the chocolate into a heatproof bowl. Pour in the cream and stir once or twice.
2 Set the bowl over a pan of gently simmering water, add the ginger and syrup, corn syrup, and butter. Let melt, stirring once or twice to combine. Set aside until cooled to room temperature.
3 When cool, beat the mixture with an electric mixer until soft, fluffy, and paler in color. Beat in the whisky briefly. Pour into a lightly oiled disposable foil container (7 inches x 5 inches) and refrigerate to set.
4 Lay out a large piece of parchment paper on your counter and dust liberally with cocoa powder.
5 Retrieve the foil container from the refrigerator and snip its edges so that you can carefully peel them away. Turn out the truffle block onto a board. Cut into 1¼-inch cubes (you'll need to clean the knife with paper towels every few cuts) and transfer the truffles to the cocoa-covered parchment paper as you go.
6 Dust the truffles with yet more cocoa powder and roll, pressing gently, to cover completely.
7 Transfer the truffles to petit-four paper cups and arrange in lidded boxes. Store in the refrigerator, where they can last for up to two weeks.

CHOCOLATE PEPPERMINT CRISP

PREPARATION: *20 minutes,*
 plus setting
COOKING: *5 minutes*
MAKES: *9oz*

7oz semisweet chocolate, broken
 into pieces
¼ cup light brown sugar, plus
 extra for sprinkling
1½ tsp peppermint extract
sunflower oil, for greasing

Deliciously moreish yet so simple to make, these after-dinner nibbles can be made in a variety of flavors using other good-quality extracts, such as orange, cinnamon, or coffee, as you wish.

1 Put the chocolate into a heatproof bowl set over a pan of gently simmering water. Let melt, stirring once or twice until smooth. Let the melted chocolate cool slightly.

2 In a small bowl, mix together the sugar and peppermint extract. Stir into the cooled chocolate.

3 Pour onto a marble slab (or onto a lightly oiled cookie sheet) and spread the chocolate out into a square about 9 inches in size. Let set for a few minutes, then sprinkle over a spoonful of the sugar to decorate (if you do this too soon, the sugar will dissolve and the chocolate won't be crunchy).

4 When the chocolate has hardened, cut into randomly sized pieces. The peppermint crisp will keep for up to a month wrapped or in an airtight container, stored in a cool place.

Waxed paper parcels can be personalized with string and a label —simple but stylish.

TIFFIN

PREPARATION: *30 minutes,*
   plus chilling
COOKING: *5 minutes*
MAKES: *36 squares*

generous 5 tbsp unsalted butter
⅔ cup corn syrup
1 tbsp brandy (optional)
½ cup unsweetened cocoa
   powder
7oz shortbread, roughly chopped
generous ½ cup raisins
scant ½ cup hazelnuts, toasted
10½oz milk chocolate, broken
   into pieces

A small piece of this nutty cookie-like "cake" delivers an intense chocolate hit, so you can cut it up into small pieces—perfect for serving as a petit four with an after-dinner coffee.

1 Line an 8-inch square pan with parchment paper. Gently melt the butter and syrup in a pan, stirring to combine.
2 Put the remaining ingredients, except for the chocolate, into a bowl and mix well. Pour in the butter and syrup mixture and stir until thoroughly combined.
3 Pour into the prepared pan and level. Chill until solid.
4 Put the chocolate pieces into a heatproof bowl set over a pan of gently simmering water. Let melt, stirring once or twice until smooth. Pour evenly over the cookie base and let set at room temperature.
5 Once set, cut into ¾–1¼-inch squares. This tiffin keeps for up to two weeks in an airtight container.

PANFORTE

I like the diminutive version of this rich Italian confection; and, of course, it means you'll have more to give away. You can, if you prefer, make a larger version (using an 8-inch pan) and cut into wedges before wrapping; if you do, you'll need to increase the baking time to 1 hour.

PREPARATION: **45 minutes**
COOKING: **1 hour**
MAKES: **4 cakes of 4 inches**

scant 1 cup each of pistachios and hazelnuts
vegetable oil, for greasing
3⅔ cups candied peel
½ tsp ground cinnamon
¼ tsp each of ground allspice, nutmeg, coriander, and white pepper
scant ½ cup all-purpose flour
¼ cup unsweetened cocoa powder
½ cup granulated sugar
½ cup liquid honey
confectioners' sugar, for dredging

1 Preheat the oven to 350°F, and have a couple of dessert spoons and a cup of hot water handy.

2 Spread the nuts onto a cookie sheet and bake for 10 minutes until lightly golden. Remove from the oven, cool, then roughly chop.

3 Lower the temperature to 300°F. Grease and line the bases of four 4-inch springform cake pans with parchment paper.

4 Put the peel, spices, flour, and cocoa into a large bowl along with the nuts. Stir to combine. Keep warm while you make the sugar syrup.

5 Heat the sugar and honey gently in a small pan until the sugar has dissolved. Then bring to a boil and cook until it reaches 250°F (the hard ball stage) on a candy thermometer. If you don't have a thermometer, drop a teaspoon of the mixture into a bowl of cold water. Bring it together with your fingers—it should form a hard ball.

6 Working quickly, stir the sugar syrup into the flour mixture. Wet a couple of dessert spoons and use them to transfer the mixture into the cake pans. Press down firmly. Be patient—the mixture is sticky.

7 Bake the panforte in a preheated oven for 35 to 40 minutes.

8 Remove from the oven and cool on a wire rack. Slide a knife around the edges to loosen. Remove from the pans, peel away the parchment, and dredge the tops of the panforte with confectioners' sugar. I find it's best wrapped in cellophane. This panforte keeps for up to two months when wrapped or stored in an airtight container.

The delights of chocolate   107

CHOCOLATE KISSES

PREPARATION: *40 minutes, plus chilling*
COOKING: **10 minutes**
MAKES: **16**

3½oz milk chocolate, broken into
  pieces
3½oz semisweet chocolate,
  broken into pieces
2 tbsp butter
5 tbsp heavy cream
1 tsp rose water
1 tsp violet liqueur or violet
  extract
crystallized rose petals and
  violets, to decorate

Never out of fashion, floral creams are just dreamy. These are my twist on the classic rose and violet creams that my grandmother adored.

1 Arrange 16 foil petit-four foil cups on a tray or cookie sheet. Melt the milk chocolate in a heatproof bowl set over a pan of gently simmering water, stirring once or twice until smooth.

2 Spoon a little chocolate into each cup and, using a small paintbrush, paint the insides of the cup. Let set in the refrigerator.

3 Repeat step 2 twice more and then let set completely, preferably overnight. Then, very carefully peel away the foil cups.

4 Put the semisweet chocolate and butter in a bowl. Put the cream in a small pan and bring to a boil, pour over the chocolate and butter. Set this bowl over a pan of gently simmering water and stir once or twice until the chocolate has completely melted. Set aside until cooled to room temperature.

5 Beat the chocolate mixture until light and fluffy. Divide into two and add the rose water to one half and the violet liqueur to the other.

6 Fill a pastry bag fitted with a star tip and pipe a swirl of the chocolate rose mixture into half of the chocolate cups. Top with a crystallized rose petal. Repeat with the violet mixture and top with a crystallized violet.

7 Transfer the chocolates into new foil cups. These chocolates keep for up to a week chilled but they're best enjoyed at room temperature.

RIGHT *A delightful selection of Chocolate kisses with crystallized rose and violet petals, and Salted caramel cups. Coffee anyone?*

SALTED CARAMEL CUPS

PREPARATION: *50 minutes,*
plus chilling
COOKING: *20 minutes*
MAKES: 16

6¼oz semisweet chocolate,
  broken into pieces
generous ¼ cup superfine sugar
1 tbsp water
scant ¼ cup heavy cream
1 tbsp unsalted butter
¼–½ tsp salt
gold edible sprinkles, to decorate
  (optional)

The dreamy combination of salt and sweet is hard to beat. Here I pair the two in dainty cases. They're the perfect size to pop in your mouth.

1 Arrange 16 foil petit-four foil cups on a tray or cookie sheet. Melt 3½oz of the chocolate in a heatproof bowl set over a pan of gently simmering water, stirring once or twice until smooth.

2 Spoon a little chocolate into each cup and, using a small paintbrush, paint the insides of the cup. Let set in the refrigerator.

3 Repeat step 2 twice more and then let set completely, preferably overnight. Then, very carefully peel away the foil cups.

4 Heat the sugar and water in a small deep pan until the sugar has dissolved. Brush the sides with a wet pastry brush to dissolve any stray sugar crystals. Boil for 5 to 6 minutes until the syrup is deep amber.

5 Remove from the heat and stir in the cream—be aware that it will bubble up, but keep stirring. Stir in the butter and salt. Set the caramel aside to cool to room temperature.

6 Fill the cups with the caramel. Chill until firm.

7 Melt the remaining chocolate as in step 1. Smooth a layer of chocolate across the caramel to seal. Sprinkle with gold decorations and chill.

8 Transfer the chocolates into clean petit-four foil cups. These caramel cups keep for up to a week chilled but they're best savored when served at room temperature.

Create a selection of chocolates and truffles for a favorite chocoholic friend.

CHOCOLATE FUDGE SAUCE

PREPARATION: *20 minutes*
COOKING: *about 10 minutes*
MAKES: *about 1lb 3½oz*

If you can stop yourself eating this rich and decadent chocolate sauce straight from the jar (it's hard, I can tell you!), then it's perfectly joyous melted and poured over ice cream.

1¼ *cups heavy cream*
½ *cup light brown sugar*
2 *tbsp corn syrup*
2 *tbsp unsalted butter*
7oz *semisweet chocolate, broken*
  into pieces
1 *tsp vanilla extract*
a tiny pinch of salt

1 Put the cream, sugar, syrup, and butter into a pan. Heat gently, stirring, until the sugar has dissolved.
2 Bring to a boil and bubble gently for 4 minutes until thickened. Remove from the heat, add the chocolate, and stir until melted and thoroughly combined.
3 Stir in the vanilla and salt. Then, pour into sterilized containers, seal, and label. This sauce keeps for up to two weeks in the refrigerator. To use, heat gently in a pan, stirring, until melted.

SMOKY NUTS

PREPARATION: **10 minutes**
COOKING: **10 minutes**
MAKES: **2 cups**

**2 cups mixed nuts, such as
cashews, blanched almonds,
macadamias, and brazil nuts**
1 tbsp olive oil
1 tsp sea salt
1 tsp smoked paprika

These nuts look fantastic packaged simply
in cellophane with ribbon or tape or in a
compartmentalized box. If you or a friend likes
their nuts spicier, then simply add in a couple of
pinches of chile powder with the paprika.

1 Preheat the oven to 350°F.
2 Toss the nuts together or each type separately in the
oil, depending on how you want to package them. Roast
in a preheated oven for 5 to 10 minutes until golden.
3 Remove from the oven, then immediately toss in the
salt and paprika, and let cool.
4 These flavorsome nuts keep for up to two weeks in
an airtight container or sealed plastic bag.

Package these in cellophane bags or a
box divided into separate compartments.

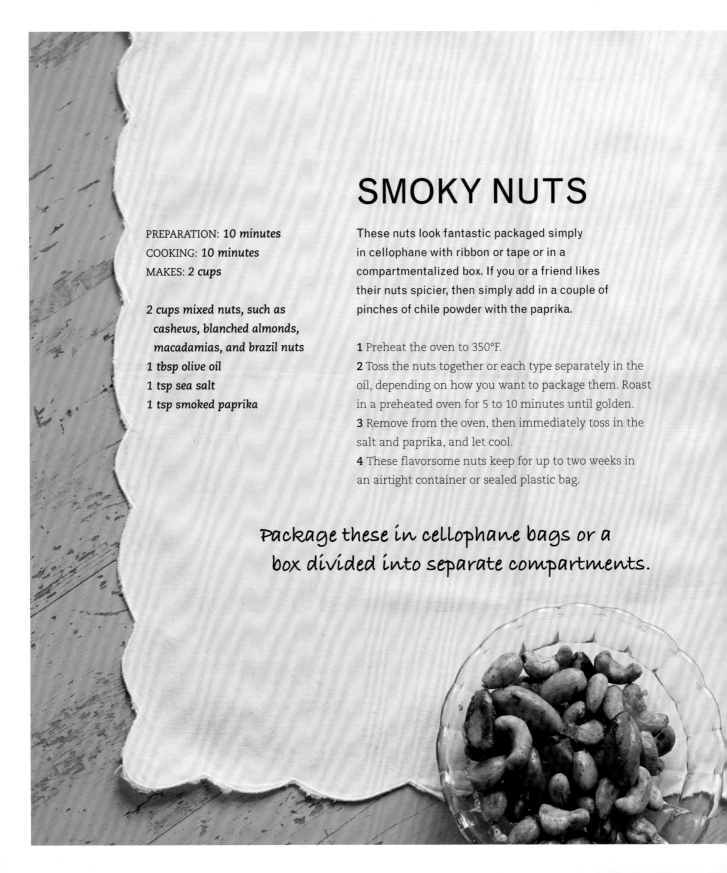

SPICY SEEDS

PREPARATION: **5 minutes**
COOKING: **10 to 15 minutes**
MAKES: *about 2½ cups*

scant ½ cup sesame seeds
scant 1 cup sunflower seeds
scant 1 cup pumpkin seeds
1 tsp salt
½ tsp garam masala powder
1½ tbsp sunflower oil

These spicy seeds make an unusual and ever-so-useful savory gift to nibble on or sprinkle onto salads. You can vary the seed mix to match the preferences of the person you have in mind for the gift.

1 Preheat the oven to 400°F and line a cookie sheet with parchment paper.
2 Meanwhile, mix together all of the ingredients until everything is coated well.
3 Tip them out and spread into one layer on the prepared cookie sheet. Bake in a preheated oven for 10 to 15 minutes, turning once or twice, until golden.
4 Remove from the oven, let cool on the cookie sheet, and pack into sterilized jars. Seal the jars and label. These seeds keep for up to four weeks.

CHEESE STRAWS

PREPARATION: **15 minutes,**
  plus chilling
COOKING: **15 minutes**
MAKES: **12**

11¼oz ready-rolled puff pastry
milk, for brushing
6 tbsp finely grated Parmesan
  cheese
sesame seeds and poppy seeds,
  for sprinkling (optional)

1 Preheat the oven to 425°F, and line two to three cookie sheets with parchment paper.
2 Carefully unroll the pastry sheet and trim the edges to neaten. Cut the pastry into four equal pieces, then cut each quarter into strips ¾-inch wide.
3 Brush each strip of pastry with milk and sprinkle them with the cheese. Give each strip a couple of twists, then arrange on the cookie sheets. If you like, sprinkle some straws with sesame or poppy seeds, then chill for 20 minutes.
4 Bake in a preheated oven for 10 to 15 minutes until golden. Remove from the oven and transfer to wire racks to cool. These cheese straws keep for up to two weeks in an airtight container or sealed plastic bag.

These moreish melt-in-the-mouth morsels can be whipped up in no time since they use ready-rolled pastry. Why not make some to take to a friend's for dinner or package up as a special savory treat?

POPPY AND SESAME SEED CRACKERS

1 Sift the flour and baking powder into a bowl with the salt. Rub in the butter to give fine bread crumbs; do this in a food processor, if you like.

2 Stir in the seeds. Sprinkle over the water and bring together the mixture with a flat-bladed knife to form a firm dough. Knead briefly until smooth. Flatten into a disc, wrap in plastic wrap, and chill for 20 minutes, so it will be firm enough to roll easily.

3 Meanwhile, preheat the oven to 350°F, and lightly grease two or three cookie sheets.

4 Roll out the dough on a lightly floured counter to a thickness of ⅛ inch. Stamp out squares with a 2½-inch fluted cutter, cutting them close together and re-rolling any trimmings. Arrange on the cookie sheets and prick all over with a fork.

5 Bake for 10 to 15 minutes until the edges are pale golden and crisp. If any of the crackers puff up, push down gently with the back of a spoon.

6 Remove from the oven and cool on a wire rack. These crackers keep for up to two weeks in an airtight container.

2 cups all-purpose flour, plus extra
  for dusting
1 tsp baking powder
½ tsp salt
scant ¼ cup unsalted butter, diced,
  plus extra for greasing
1 tbsp poppy seeds
1 tbsp sesame seeds
4–5 tbsp cold water

PREPARATION: *20 minutes,*
  plus chilling
COOKING: *15 minutes*
MAKES: *25 to 30*

These make a perfect gift for any fromageophiles in your life. Why not make up a mini hamper or basket with some fruit cheese (see page 80), pickled onions (see page 78), or a chutney (see page 74) for the ultimate cheeseboard accompaniment?

ROASTED BABY BELL PEPPERS

PREPARATION: *35 minutes*
COOKING: *20 minutes*
MAKES: *about 1lb 11¾oz*

1lb 2oz baby bell peppers (or an
*   equal weight of full-sized bell*
*   peppers)*
1 tbsp white wine vinegar
2 sprigs thyme, leaves picked
1 tsp fennel seeds
extra-virgin olive oil

These beautiful little peppers
liven up no end of dishes, from
salads to antipasti, or simply
serve as a predinner nibble.

1 Preheat the oven to 400°F. Put the peppers in one layer in a rimmed
baking sheet and roast for 20 to 25 minutes until lightly charred.
2 Immediately transfer the peppers to a large plastic bag and tie the
ends together. Leave the peppers to sit in the bag for 10 minutes—the
steam in the bag will loosen their skins.
3 When the peppers are cool enough to handle, peel away the skins. I try
to keep the stalks intact as they look pretty when kept whole in the jar.
4 Put the peeled peppers in a large bowl with the vinegar, thyme, fennel
seeds, and any juices from the bag. Gently mix together.
5 Transfer to sterilized jars and cover the peppers completely with olive
oil. Seal the jars and label. These peppers keep for up to three months.
Once opened, chill and consume within two weeks.

SWEDISH CRISPBREADS

PREPARATION: *20 minutes,*
    plus rising
COOKING: *20 minutes*
MAKES: 20

2 cups rye flour, plus extra for
    dusting
¾ cup white bread flour
1 tsp active dry yeast
1 tbsp caraway seeds
½ tsp salt
¾–1 cup lukewarm water

To make authentic Swedish crispbreads, I use my knobbly Knäckebröd rolling pin, which is especially made for the job.

1 Put the flours, yeast, seeds, and salt in a large bowl. Make a well in the center and add enough of the water to make a firm dough.
2 Turn out onto a lightly floured counter and knead for 10 minutes until smooth and elastic. Alternatively, use the dough hook on a stand mixer for 7 minutes. Cover and let rise for 45 minutes.
3 Divide the dough into 20 pieces and roll into balls. Meanwhile, preheat the oven to 455°F.
4 Generously dust the counter with rye flour and roll out each ball to a 4¼-inch circle; if you don't have a Knäckebröd rolling pin and you're using a regular rolling pin, then simply prick all over with a fork.
5 Bake in a preheated oven in several batches for 2 to 5 minutes until brown and crisp. Remove from the oven and cool on wire rack. These crispbreads keep for up to two months in an airtight container.

SWEET WHOLE WHEAT CRACKERS

PREPARATION: *30 minutes,*
  plus chilling
COOKING: **20 to 25 minutes**
MAKES: *about 35*

3½ cups whole wheat flour
2 cups fine oatmeal
1 tbsp baking powder
½ cup plus 1 tbsp superfine
  sugar
¾ cup butter, diced
scant ⅔ cup milk

This most wonderfully versatile cracker (like a Graham cracker) can be enjoyed with a cup of tea or with soft cheese as part of a cheeseboard. So, from a gift-giving point of view, it's an all-round winner.

1 Preheat the oven to 350°F, and lightly grease two or three cookie sheets.
2 Put the flour, oatmeal, baking powder, and sugar into a large mixing bowl and rub in the butter until it resembles bread crumbs—you could do this in a food processor if you prefer.
3 Using a flat-bladed knife, add enough milk to the crumbs to make a soft dough. Then, bring together with your hands and knead gently until smooth. Shape into a disc, wrap in plastic wrap, and let rest for 20 minutes (put it in the refrigerator to rest if the kitchen is warm).
4 Roll out the dough on a lightly floured counter to a thickness of ¼ inch. Cut out circles with a 2½–2¾-inch cutter, re-rolling any trimmings. Arrange on the cookie sheets and prick a few times with a fork. Bake in a preheated oven for 20 to 25 minutes.
5 Remove from the oven and cool for a couple of minutes on the sheets before transferring to wire racks to cool. These crackers keep for up to a month in an airtight container or sealed plastic bag.

BLUE CHEESE AND SAGE MUFFINS

PREPARATION: *10 minutes*

COOKING: *20 minutes*

MAKES: *12*

Make these muffins for the friend in your life who prefers savory treats. For a milder flavor, I've found they also work well with a hard cheese, such as Cheddar.

1¾ cups all-purpose flour

1½ cups cornmeal

2 tbsp baking powder

2 tbsp finely chopped sage leaves

½ tsp salt

4 medium eggs

1⅔ cups whole milk

scant ¼ cup sunflower oil

3½oz blue cheese, crumbled

1 Preheat the oven to 425°F, and then line a 12-hole muffin tin with paper liners.

2 Put the flour, cornmeal, baking powder, sage, and salt into a large bowl. Make a well in the center.

3 Beat together the eggs, milk, and oil in a large pitcher. Pour this mixture into the dry ingredients and stir together until well combined. Lastly, stir in the cheese. It's quite a sloppy batter so don't panic.

4 Divide the batter among the muffin liners and bake for 20 to 25 minutes until golden and risen. Remove from the oven and cool completely on a wire rack before wrapping. These muffins are best eaten within two days.

LEMON AND FENNEL OIL

PREPARATION: **10 minutes,
plus standing**
MAKES: **2½ cups**

2½ cups good-quality extra-
virgin olive oil
1 tsp fennel seeds, lightly
crushed
finely grated zest 1 unwaxed
lemon
fennel herb sprig, to finish
(optional)
wide strip of lemon peel, to
finish (optional)

1 Put the ingredients into a large pitcher or bowl. Cover with a lid
or plastic wrap, and leave in a cool, dark place for a month, swirling
the oil occasionally.
2 Strain the oil into sterilized bottles. Add a sprig of fresh fennel herb
and a strip of lemon peel to each bottle, if you like. Seal and label.
Store in a cool, dry place out of sunlight for up to six months.

This wonderfully aromatic
oil has myriad uses, but
I like to use it in salad
dressings or in a marinade
for fish or poultry.

MARINATED OLIVES

PREPARATION: *20 minutes,*
plus marinating
MAKES: *about 1⅓ cups of each*
flavor

4 cups green or black olives or a
mixture of both, drained
1½ cups olive oil
scant ⅔ cups white wine vinegar
12 garlic cloves, sliced thinly

FOR GREEK OLIVES:
2 sprigs each oregano and
thyme
2 slices lemon, cut into small
wedges

If I'm invited to friends for dinner, I like to take along a pot of these marinated olives as a gift for the host—it makes a welcome change from flowers or chocolates.

1 Divide the olives among three non-metallic bowls. Divide the oil, vinegar, and garlic among each set of olives.
2 Stir in each flavoring. Cover and let marinate overnight.
3 Decant into sterilized jars, seal, and label. Keep chilled and use any version of these marinated olives within two weeks.

FOR ITALIAN OLIVES:
2 sprigs rosemary
1 tsp fennel seeds
1 tsp mixed peppercorns

FOR MIDDLE EASTERN OLIVES:
1 tsp each cumin and coriander
seeds
finely grated zest of 1 lemon and
1 orange

MARINATED GOAT CHEESE

PREPARATION: *20 minutes*
MAKES: *about 1lb 2oz*

10½oz goat cheese, cubed
1½ cups green olives
thyme or rosemary sprigs
fresh bay leaves
few wide strips of lemon zest
extra-virgin olive oil

Transform store-bought goat cheese into something truly special. It's delicious eaten on its own, but can enliven any salad or pizza and equally sits right at home on a platter of antipasti. I've found this recipe also works well with feta cheese.

1 Fill sterilized jars two-thirds full with the goat cheese and olives. Tuck in a herb sprig, bay leaf, and piece of lemon zest.
2 Top up with the olive oil, making sure the cheese and olives are covered. Seal and label. Chill and eat within two weeks.

ROSEMARY GRISSINI

PREPARATION: *30 minutes,*
  plus rising
COOKING: *15 minutes*
MAKES: *24*

3¼ cups white bread flour
2 tbsp finely chopped rosemary
½ tsp salt
1 tsp active dry yeast
3 tbsp olive oil, plus extra for
  greasing and brushing
generous ¾ cup lukewarm water

Breadsticks—or as the Italians say "grissini"—are hard to beat for nibbling or dipping, and homemade ones, with their lovely "each one is slightly different" appeal, make great gifts. Partner them with one or more of the items in my Italian kit (see page 165).

1 Put the flour, rosemary, and salt into a large bowl and stir in the yeast. Make a well in the center and pour in the olive oil and enough warm water to make a soft but not too sticky dough.
2 Lightly flour a counter and knead the dough for 10 minutes until smooth and elastic. Transfer the dough to a lightly oiled bowl, cover with a dish towel, and let rise in a warm place for 1½ hours, until doubled in size.
3 Meanwhile, preheat the oven to 425°F, and lightly oil two to three large cookie sheets.
4 Divide the dough into 24 equal pieces (about 1¼ ounces in weight) and roll each one under your fingers to form a long thin "sausage" (about 12 inches long). Arrange these "sausages" spaced apart on the cookie sheets and brush with some oil.
5 Bake in a preheated oven for 12 to 15 minutes until golden and hollow sounding. Remove from the oven and transfer to a wire rack to cool completely. These grissini keep for three days in an airtight container.

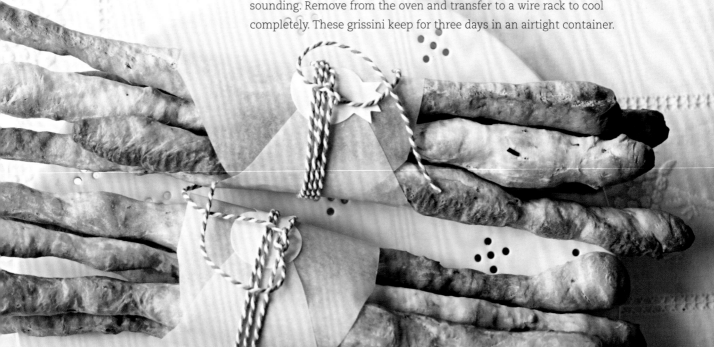

Raise a
glass

VANILLA CARAMEL LIQUEUR

PREPARATION: *15 minutes,
plus standing*
MAKES: *about 1 pint 6fl oz*

5½oz soft vanilla caramels
1 pint 6fl oz vodka

This gloriously sweet nectar will tickle anyone's tastebuds. You can use this same method to flavor vodka with a variety of candies, such as jelly beans or babies, Turkish delight, or butterscotch. It's a perfect drink to personalize with someone's favorite candies.

1 Put the caramels into a wide-necked sealable jar. Pour over the vodka and allow the caramels to dissolve slowly. Seal the jar and store in a dark, cool place. Leave to infuse for a week, shaking every day to ensure the caramels are totally dissolved. (If you don't have the time, you can melt the caramels instead. Simply put the caramels in a heatproof bowl set over a pan of gently simmering water and leave to melt. Then, carefully transfer the liquid caramel into the jar and stir in the vodka. Seal and store as above.)
2 Decant the liqueur into sterilized bottles, seal, and label. This bottle of loveliness keeps indefinitely. Shake well before using, as some caramels can cause it to separate on standing.

Decant into an unusual bottle, which can be reused and enjoyed again and again.

CRÈME DE CASSIS

PREPARATION: *15 minutes,*
  plus standing
MAKES: *about 1¾ pints*

5 cups blackcurrants, de-stalked
2 whole cloves
1 small cinnamon stick
1⅓ cups granulated sugar
1 pint 6fl oz vodka or eau de vie

For an extra-special gift, pair this liqueur with a bottle of sparkling wine to make the classic Kir Royale.

1 Put the fruit and spices into a wide-necked sealable jar. Cover with the sugar, then pour over the vodka or eau de vie—by the way, the alcohol doesn't need to be expensive or top quality.
2 Seal the jar and store in a dark, cool place. Shake every day for the first week to dissolve the sugar, then just a couple of times a week. Leave to infuse for at least a month, but the longer you can bear to wait, the better it will taste.
3 Strain the fruit and liqueur through a cheesecloth-lined sieve into a large pitcher. Decant the liqueur into sterilized bottles, seal, and label. This liqueur keeps indefinitely, although it's unlikely to last long.

REDCURRANT GIN

PREPARATION: *15 minutes,*
plus standing
MAKES: *about 1¾ pints*

3½ *cups redcurrants, de-stalked*
1½ *cups granulated sugar*
1⅓ *pints gin*

This glorious ruby-red liqueur is great whether drunk as a small measure or topped up with soda as a long drink. De-stalking currants can be fiddly and I find pulling a fork down the stem releases them nicely. Don't worry, as you will be straining the liqueur after infusing.

1 Put the fruit into a wide-necked sealable jar. Cover with the sugar, then pour over the gin. By the way, the alcohol doesn't need to be expensive or top quality.
2 Seal the jar and store in a dark, cool place. Shake daily for the first week to dissolve the sugar, then twice a week. Leave to infuse for at least a month, but the longer you can wait the better it will taste.
3 Strain the fruit and liqueur through a cheesecloth-lined sieve into a large pitcher. Decant the liqueur into sterilized bottles, seal, and label. This liqueur keeps indefinitely. If you like, you can reward your efforts by eating the infused fruit, perhaps with a scoop of vanilla ice cream and a drizzle of the liqueur.

LEMON SCHNAPPS

Don't keep this citrus liqueur just for sipping on its own; it tastes just wonderful when mixed with tonic for a long drink.

PREPARATION: *30 minutes*
MAKES: *about 1¾ pints*

6 *large unwaxed lemons*
1 *pint 6fl oz schnapps*
1¼ *cups granulated sugar*
generous ¾ cup water

1 Peel the rind away from the lemons with a vegetable peeler, making sure that you leave behind the bitter white pith.
2 Put the peel into a wide-necked sealable jar or bowl. Cover with the schnapps, seal or cover with plastic wrap, and leave in a cool, dark place for a week.
3 Heat the sugar and water gently in a pan to dissolve the sugar.
4 Strain the schnapps through a cheesecloth-lined sieve, discarding the lemon peel. Stir in the sugar syrup.
5 Decant the liqueur into sterilized bottles, seal, and label. Leave for at least two weeks before drinking, but the longer you leave it the better it tastes. This schnapps keeps indefinitely. I like to keep mine in the freezer.

COFFEE CREAM LIQUEUR

Serve this creamy, rich liqueur neat over ice or drizzle over ice cream for an indulgent after-dinner treat.

1 Put the coffee beans and whisky in a bowl, cover, and let infuse overnight.
2 Heat the condensed milk and chocolate gently in a small pan, stirring once or twice, until the chocolate has melted.
3 Strain the whisky and put into a blender or food processor with the condensed milk and chocolate. Whiz for a minute or two to blend thoroughly, transfer to a bowl, and chill overnight.
4 Remove any skin that might have formed during chilling and decant into sterilized bottles, seal, and label. This superb tipple keeps for up to a month in the refrigerator.

PREPARATION: *30 minutes,*
  plus infusing and chilling
MAKES: *about 1¾ pints*

1¾oz coffee beans
1 pint whisky
14oz canned sweetened condensed
  milk
1½oz semisweet chocolate, broken
  into pieces

LE VIN D'ORANGE

This Provençal aperitif is traditionally made with Seville oranges. If you are making this when these wonderfully bitter oranges are in season, simply omit the lemon juice.

1 Blanch the whole oranges in boiling water for 3 minutes to kill off the natural yeasts on the surface that might cause fermentation. Drain.
2 Halve and squeeze the oranges. Put the juice and shells into a large bowl or sealable jar along with the remaining ingredients. Cover and let infuse for at least a month.
3 Strain through a cheesecloth-lined sieve into a large pitcher. Decant into sterilized bottles, seal, and label. This liqueur keeps indefinitely.

PREPARATION: *15 minutes, plus standing*
COOKING: *3 minutes*
MAKES: *about 1¾ pints*

3 large juicy oranges
juice 1 lemon
scant 1 cup granulated sugar
3¼ cups rosé wine
scant ⅔ cup vodka or eau de vie
1 vanilla bean, split and scraped

GOLDEN VODKA

PREPARATION: *20 minutes,*
 plus infusing
MAKES: *1 pint 6fl oz*

2 vanilla beans, split
1 pint 6fl oz vodka
2 sheets gold leaf (mine were
 2 inches square)

Who could fail to be impressed by this sumptuous golden vodka that reveals a special surprise when it's given a shake?

1 Pop the vanilla beans into the bottle of vodka and leave to infuse for at least a week. The vodka will steadily become a wondrous golden color and will smell delightfully aromatic.

2 Remove the vanilla beans—you could wash and dry them and use to flavor some superfine sugar if you like. Next, decant the vodka into your chosen sterilized gift bottles.

3 Gold leaf is incredibly delicate, so carefully pick up small flakes (do this on the paper it comes in) with a small, slightly damp paintbrush and drop into the bottle. (Don't worry if it blobs up as it gets wet because as soon as you drop it into the vodka it will expand into a flake again—watch it, it's magical!) Seal the bottles and label. This golden nectar keeps indefinitely.

Watch friends and family
marvel at its magical
appearance, with glittering
gold flakes dancing
around in the light.

ROSE AND LIME SYRUP

PREPARATION: *30 minutes*
COOKING: *10 minutes*
MAKES: *about 1 pint 18½fl oz*

4½ cups granulated sugar
¼ tsp cream of tartar
1 vanilla bean, split
finely grated zest and juice of
   3 limes
5 cups water
2 tsp rose water

A versatile syrup that can be used in cocktails, drizzled over pancakes or ice cream, or simply diluted with sparkling water for a wonderfully refreshing summery drink.

1 Put the sugar, cream of tartar, vanilla bean, and lime zest in a large pan with the water. Heat gently to dissolve the sugar then bring to a boil and bubble for 5 minutes until syrupy. Set aside to infuse for 30 minutes.
2 Strain the sugar syrup through a cheesecloth-lined sieve. Stir in the lime juice and rose water. Taste and add more rose water if necessary.
3 Decant into sterilized bottles, seal, and label. This syrup keeps for four weeks in the refrigerator.

RHUBARB AND GINGER CORDIAL

PREPARATION: *25 minutes*
COOKING: *15 minutes*
MAKES: *about 1¾ pints*

2¼lb rhubarb, chopped
2 thumb-sized pieces of fresh
   ginger root, grated
1 star anise
4 cups water
granulated sugar
2 tsp citric acid

This refreshing cordial has the most glorious pink color—search out the pinkest rhubarb. As well as drinking diluted with water (fizzy or still), I like to make a rhubarb Bellini (mix 1 part cordial to 5 parts Prosecco).

1 Put the rhubarb, ginger, and star anise in a large pan with the water. Bring to a boil, then simmer for 10 minutes until the rhubarb is tender.
2 Set a sieve over a large bowl and pour in the rhubarb and juice—you'll need to do this in batches. Push down on the fruit with the back of a spoon to extract as much juice as you can. (Don't throw away the rhubarb flesh—you can sweeten it and eat with yogurt.)
3 Now, measure the volume of juice you have—you will need 1¾ cups of sugar for every 2 cups of liquid. Put the juice and sugar into a pan over low heat until the sugar has dissolved, then stir in the citric acid.
4 Strain the cordial through a cheesecloth-lined funnel into sterilized bottles. Seal and label. The cordial keeps for up to a year unopened. Once opened, store it in the refrigerator and use within two weeks.

small but
perfectly formed

MINI CHRISTMAS CAKES

PREPARATION: *45 minutes,*
  plus macerating
COOKING: *4½ hours*
MAKES: **9**

2½ *cups currants*
1¼ *cups each of golden raisins*
  and raisins
¾ *cup dried figs, diced*
zest and juice of 1 lemon
3½ *tbsp chocolate liqueur or*
  brandy
3 *sticks unsalted butter, soft,*
  plus extra for greasing
1 *cup candied peel*
½ *cup macadamia nuts, chopped*
scant ½ cup semisweet chocolate
  chips
1½ *cups dark brown sugar*
1 *tbsp molasses*
5 *medium eggs, lightly beaten*
scant 2½ cups all-purpose flour
1 *tsp mixed spice (see page 168)*
4–6 *tbsp brandy, for feeding*

TO DECORATE:
1lb 2oz *golden marzipan*
5½ *tbsp apricot jam, plus*
  1 *tbsp water*
confectioners' sugar, for dusting
2¼lb *ready-to-roll fondant icing*
edible shimmer, for dusting

1 Put the currants, golden raisins, raisins, figs, lemon zest and juice, and alcohol in a non-metallic bowl. Let macerate overnight.

2 Preheat the oven to 275°F. Grease and double line the base and sides of an 8-inch square cake pan with parchment paper. Wrap a double layer of brown paper around the pan and tie with string.

3 Stir the candied peel, nuts, and chocolate chips into the fruity batter.

4 Beat the butter and sugar with an electric mixer for about 5 minutes until fluffy and much paler in color. Then beat in the molasses.

5 Gradually beat in the eggs. If the batter looks as if it's going to curdle, beat in 1 tablespoon of flour then carry on adding the eggs.

6 Using a large metal spoon, gently fold the flour and spice into the batter until well mixed. Turn into the pan and smooth the top with the back of the spoon. Bake for 3 to 3½ hours until a skewer inserted comes out clean. Remove from the oven and cool in the pan set on a wire rack. Once cold, wrap the cake tightly in parchment paper and a layer of foil. Store in a cool, dry place, feeding it weekly with 1 tablespoon of brandy.

7 A few days before you plan to give the cakes, you will need to cover the tops with a layer of marzipan. First unwrap the cake and cut into 9 equal squares. Turn them over so that the more level bottoms become the tops. Roll out the marzipan to a ¼-inch thickness and cut out 9 squares the same size as the cake.

8 Melt the jam with the water then sieve to remove any lumps. Brush the tops of the cake with the jam. Brush away any crumbs and fix the marzipan on top. Leave in a cool place to dry out for two days.

9 When you're ready to decorate, dust a counter with confectioners' sugar and roll out the fondant icing to a ¼-inch thickness. Brush the marzipan with water, then place face down onto the icing. Carefully cut around the edges using the cake as a template. Turn the cake over and smooth the surface with the palm of your hand.

10 Stamp out Christmasy shapes with cutters and fix in place with a little water. Using a small paintbrush, dust some edible shimmer powder on top. Finish off with a ribbon and secure. Wrap in cellophane and tie with more ribbon. This cake keeps for up to two months.

My friends and family love these Christmas cakes in miniature. Sometimes, eating a full-sized version can seem overwhelming and can stretch on into the New Year, so my solution is to scale it down into a more manageable—and I have to say cute—size. You'll need to make the large cake at least four to six weeks before you divide it into smaller versions to decorate, because the flavor needs time to mature. Be warned, you will need a very large bowl to accommodate all the cake batter—I have one that is brought out only once a year just for this job.

HAZELNUT BROWNIES

Anything in miniature is somehow irresistible and the same rings true for these nutty brownies. I dare you to find someone who could resist these rich, chocolately, nutty squares.

PREPARATION: *35 minutes*
COOKING: *25 minutes*
MAKES: *28*

2½ sticks butter, plus extra for greasing
9oz semisweet chocolate, broken into pieces
3 medium eggs, separated
1 cup superfine sugar
2 tbsp milk
2 tsp instant coffee dissolved in 1 tbsp boiling water
½ cup plus 1 tbsp self-rising flour
3 cups hazelnuts, toasted and chopped
generous ½ cup semisweet chocolate chips

1 Preheat the oven to 375°F, and grease and line an 11-inch x 7-inch baking pan with parchment paper.
2 Melt the chocolate pieces with the butter in a heatproof bowl set over gently simmering water. Cool slightly and meanwhile beat together the egg yolks, sugar, milk, and coffee, and then the cooled chocolate. Fold in the flour using a metal spoon, followed by the nuts and chocolate chips.
3 In a separate bowl, beat the egg whites until stiff and gently fold into the batter. Carefully pour into the prepared pan and bake in a preheated oven for 20–25 minutes until just firm to the touch—a skewer inserted into the brownie should still have a little batter clinging to it. You want the brownies to be moist, not dry.
4 Remove from the oven and let cool in the pan, then turn out and mark into squares when completely cold. These brownies keep for up to two weeks in an airtight container or sealed plastic bag.

MOCHA MUFFINS

A super-easy bake, muffins always meet with delighted faces when given as a gift. Here the coffee brings out the richness of the cocoa.

PREPARATION: *20 minutes*
COOKING: *15 minutes*
MAKES: *24*

scant 1 cup superfine sugar
1¾ cups self-rising flour
½ cup unsweetened cocoa
  powder
2 tsp instant coffee dissolved in
  1 tbsp boiling water
1 cup milk

½ cup sunflower oil
2 medium eggs, beaten

FOR THE FROSTING:
5 cups confectioners' sugar,
  sifted
2–3 tbsp hot water
few drops of coffee extract
chocolate coffee beans, to
  decorate (optional)

1 Preheat the oven to 400°F, and then line two 12-hole mini muffin tins with paper liners.
2 Sift together the dry ingredients into a large bowl and make a well in the center. In another bowl, add the milk and oil to the eggs and pour into the well. Quickly mix together and divide among the liners.
3 Bake in a preheated oven for 15 minutes, then remove from the oven and cool on a wire rack.
4 Mix together the confectioners' sugar with the hot water and the coffee extract to make a spreadable frosting. Decorate the muffins and top with a bean, if using. These muffins keep for two to three days in an airtight container or sealed plastic bag.

MINI LEBKUCHEN

PREPARATION: *25 minutes,*
  plus cooling
COOKING: *12 minutes*
MAKES: *35 to 38*

scant ½ stick butter
2 tbsp milk
⅔ cup liquid honey
1¾ cups all-purpose flour
2 tbsp cornstarch
½ tsp each of ground coriander,
  ground ginger, ground
  cardamom (from about 6 pods),
  and ground cinnamon
1 tsp baking soda

TO FINISH:
3 tbsp butter, melted
1 tbsp each superfine sugar and
  confectioners' sugar mixed
  together

Lebkuchen are a traditional baked Christmas treat in Germany; think of it a bit like gingerbread. I find the wonderful spice flavors improve with keeping, so make them at least a week before giving your gift.

1 Put the butter, milk, and honey in a large pan and heat gently. Stir to combine and take off the heat.
2 Sift the flours, spices, and baking soda together in a bowl. Tip into the honeyed milk and mix until smooth. Cover and let cool for a few hours.
3 Preheat the oven to 350°F, and grease two or three cookie sheets.
4 Take teaspoon heaps of the batter and roll into walnut-sized balls. Arrange on the cookie sheets, spaced well apart.
5 Bake in a preheated oven for 10 to 12 minutes.
6 Remove from the oven, let cool for a minute or so, and then brush each cookie with melted butter and dust with the sugar mix. Cool completely on a wire rack. These cookies keep for a month in an airtight container or sealed plastic bag.

FLORENTINES

PREPARATION: *25 minutes*
COOKING: *40 minutes*
MAKES: *28 to 30*

*scant ½ stick butter, plus extra
  for greasing*
¼ cup golden superfine sugar
2 tbsp heavy cream
¼ cup cranberries
*½ cup slivered almonds, roughly
  chopped*
⅓ cup mixed candied peel
¼ cup stem ginger, chopped
¼ cup pine nuts
2 tbsp all-purpose flour
*1¾oz semisweet chocolate,
  melted, to finish*

These rich, Italian-style bites are perfect with a cup of after-dinner coffee. Pine nuts aren't traditional but I find they add a pleasing crunch.

1 Preheat the oven to 350°F, and grease two to three cookie sheets.
2 Put the butter and sugar into a pan and heat gently to dissolve the sugar. Bring to a boil, take off the heat, and add the cream.
3 Beat in the rest of the ingredients. Put ½ teaspoon heaps of the mixture on the cookie sheets, spacing them well apart. Bake in batches, as you will need to work quickly when they come out of the oven.
4 Bake in a preheated oven for 8 minutes, then using a metal, round 2–2½-inch pastry cutter, quickly bring the edges of the spread cookies to the center to make a perfect round. Return to the oven for 2 to 3 minutes until a deep golden color. Let sit on the tray for 2 to 3 minutes until set, then transfer to a wire rack to cool.
5 When the cookies are cold, spread the backs with a coating of melted chocolate, then mark into wavy lines with a fork. These chewy delights keep for up to two weeks in an airtight container or sealed plastic bag.

LITTLE GEMS

PREPARATION: *45 minutes,*
  plus resting
COOKING: *10 to 15 minutes*
MAKES: *about 80*

1½ cups all-purpose flour
6 tbsp confectioners' sugar
¾ stick butter, diced
1 medium egg
1 tsp vanilla extract
14oz royal icing
flavored extracts, such as
  orange, coffee, and lemon
food coloring pastes

Transport yourself back to childhood with the sight of these super-cute and nostalgic iced cookies in miniature.

1 Sift together the flour into a bowl with the confectioners' sugar. Rub in the butter to form bread crumbs.
2 Stir in the egg and vanilla extract. Mix together with a flat-bladed knife until it clumps together. Bring together with your fingertips to form a very soft dough. Shape into a disc, wrap in plastic wrap, and chill for 1 to 2 hours until firm enough to roll. Meanwhile, preheat the oven to 375°F, and lightly grease two or three cookie sheets.
3 Unwrap the dough and roll out to a thickness of ¼ inch. Cut out bases with a 1-inch flower-shaped cutter and arrange, spaced apart, on the cookie sheets. Bake in a preheated oven for 4 to 5 minutes until golden.
4 Remove from the oven and let cool on the cookie sheets for a few minutes before transferring to a wire rack to cool.
5 Meanwhile, make up the royal icing according to the package instructions. Divide into three or four separate bowls and flavor with your chosen extracts and corresponding food colorings. Fill a pastry bag fitted with a fluted tip and pipe stars onto the cookies. Let set overnight. These little gems keep for up to a week in an airtight container or sealed plastic bag.

MERINGUE MUSHROOMS

PREPARATION: *1 hour*
COOKING: *1 hour*
MAKES: 50

4 medium egg whites, at room
  temperature
1 cup superfine sugar
melted semisweet chocolate,
  to decorate

I like to use these little meringue mushrooms to decorate my Bûche de Noël at Christmas time, but they make cute edible gifts whatever the time of year.

1 Preheat the oven to 225°F, and then line two cookie sheets with parchment paper.
2 Beat the egg whites until stiff but not dry. Beat in the sugar 1 tablespoon at a time until the meringue is thick and glossy.
3 Fill a pastry bag fitted with a large plain tip and pipe 1½-inch dome shapes onto the cookie sheets, spaced apart. Vertically pipe stem shapes alongside about 1¼-inches high. Bake in a preheated oven for 45 minutes to 1 hour until they are completely dry and they easily lift away from the parchment paper.
4 To assemble, spread the underside of the mushroom cap with chocolate. Carefully make a hole in the center with the tip of a skewer. Dip the pointed end of the stalk into the chocolate and carefully insert into the hole. Leave upside down until set (when the chocolate is almost set, score lines with a cocktail stick or toothpick to represent the gills of the mushroom). These meringue shapes keep for two weeks in an airtight container or sealed plastic bag.

LEMON SYRUP LOAF CAKES

PREPARATION: *35 minutes*
COOKING: *30 minutes*
MAKES: *8 mini loaves or*
  a 2lb loaf cake

¾ *cup butter, very soft, plus*
  extra for greasing
1½ *cups self-rising flour*
1 *tsp baking powder*
⅓ *cup cornmeal*
finely grated zest of 1 lemon
¾ *cup superfine sugar*
3 *medium eggs, lightly beaten*

FOR THE GLAZE:
¼ *cup granulated sugar*
juice of ½ lemon

Cornmeal adds a lovely crunchy texture to these mini loaves. If you can't find it in your local supermarket or deli, just increase the self-rising flour by the same amount instead.

1 Preheat the oven to 350°F, and lightly grease and line the base and sides of an 8-piece linking mini loaf pan (each loaf is 4 x 2½ x 1¼ inches) or a 2lb loaf pan (measuring 9½ x 6 x 2½ inches), with parchment paper; make sure the paper sits ½ inch above the rim of the pans. Set the pans on a cookie sheet.
2 Sift the flour and baking powder into a bowl. Stir in the cornmeal, then add the butter, lemon zest, sugar, and eggs. Beat together for 2 minutes with an electric mixer until fluffy and light in color. Divide the batter among the loaf pans and level the tops.
3 Bake in a preheated oven for 25 to 30 minutes (or 45 minutes to 1 hour for the larger loaf cake) until risen and golden, and a skewer inserted into the cakes comes out clean.
4 Remove from the oven and while the cakes are still hot, mix together the granulated sugar and lemon juice. Brush the tops of the cakes with the glaze and let cool on a wire rack for 10 minutes. Remove from the pans and peel away the parchment paper. These little loaves keep for a week in an airtight container or wrapped in cellophane.

Gifts for
the cook

BRUNCH SET

A lovely little kit for a lazy weekend brunch. A tub of fresh blueberries, bottle of maple syrup, and a packet of good coffee complete the gift.

FOR THE TROPICAL GRANOLA:

PREPARATION: *15 minutes*
COOKING: *20 minutes*
MAKES: *1lb 5oz*

2¾ *cups rolled oats*
scant ½ cup flavored liquid honey (I like orange blossom honey)
1 tbsp sunflower oil
⅔ *cup coconut flakes*
1 cup mixed chopped dried mango, pineapple, and dates

1 Preheat the oven to 350°F.
2 Put the oats into a large bowl.
3 Put the honey and oil in a small pan and very gently warm it for a minute or two—this will make it easier to mix with the oats but be careful not to boil it.
4 Pour the honey mixture into the oats and mix thoroughly until all the ingredients are coated well.
5 Spread the granola out onto a large cookie sheet. Bake for 10 minutes then stir in the coconut flakes and return to the oven for another 10 minutes until golden.
6 Remove from the oven and transfer to a bowl to cool. Then, stir in the mixed dried fruit until well combined. This granola keeps for up to a month when stored in an airtight container.

FOR THE DRIED FRUIT COMPÔTE:

PREPARATION: *5 minutes*
COOKING: *15 minutes*
SERVES: *4 to 6*

3⅓ *cups dried fruit, such as apples, pears, apricots, and prunes*
1 cinnamon stick
½ *tsp ground ginger*
3 tbsp light brown sugar
1½ *cups apple juice*

1 Put all of the ingredients into a pan and heat gently until the sugar has dissolved. Bring to a boil, then simmer for 10 to 15 minutes until syrupy.
2 Refrigerate overnight for the flavors to mingle and for the fruit to plump up. This compôte keeps for up to two weeks in the fridge. Serve at room temperature.

FOR THE PANCAKE MIX:
PREPARATION: **15 minutes**
MAKES: *about 15 pancakes*

1 cup all-purpose flour
1½ tsp baking powder
1 tbsp superfine sugar
scant ¼ cup golden raisins

1 Mix together the dry ingredients and tip into a sterilized jar. Seal. Label and attach the recipe below.

To make the pancakes: Tip the pancake mix into a large bowl. Beat in 1 medium egg and 1¼ cups of milk until smooth. Put a greased nonstick skillet over medium heat. Pour in 2 tablespoons of batter. Cook for 4 minutes until the pancake bubbles, flip, and cook for 3 minutes. Set aside, keep warm, and repeat with the remaining batter.

CHRISTMAS COOKIE KIT

1 Mix the flour with the baking powder, then tip into the jar. Shake gently to level. Spoon in the sugar and roughly level. Add the dried fruit and the chocolate chips in layers as you like.

2 Seal the jar and attach a cookie cutter, wooden spoon, and a hand-written label with the following recipe for these cookies.

CHERRY AND WHITE CHOCOLATE COOKIES

Melt generous ½ cup butter in a large pan with ⅓ cup corn syrup. Add 1 large beaten egg, then stir in the cookie mixture. Mix to form a stiff dough. Divide into two pieces, flatten into discs, and wrap in plastic wrap. Chill for 20 minutes. Preheat the oven to 350°F. Roll out the dough to a ⅛-inch thickness, stamp out shapes with the cookie cutter; transfer to greased cookie sheets. Make small holes in the top for threading cotton when baked, if you like. Bake in a preheated oven for 10 to 12 minutes until lightly golden. Cool on a wire rack; dust with confectioners' sugar. Enjoy!

4 cups all-purpose flour
2 tsp baking powder
generous ¾ cup golden superfine sugar
scant 1 cup white chocolate chips
scant 1 cup dried cranberries

PREPARATION:
15 minutes
MAKES: 25 to 30 cookies

I look out for pretty
glass storage jars and
wooden spoons at
antique centers and thrift
stores. The jar needs to
hold about 2lb. Once the
mixture has been turned
into cookies, they can be
stored in the same jar,
which is doubly pleasing.

GINGERBREAD HOUSE KIT

PREPARATION: *1½ hours*
COOKING: *10 minutes*
MAKES: *4 small houses*

3 cups all-purpose flour
1 tsp baking soda
2 tbsp ground ginger
⅔ cup butter, diced
¾ cup light brown sugar
2 tbsp corn syrup, warmed
1 medium egg, beaten
4 x 9oz white royal icing sugar,
  for the "glue"
assorted sweets, to decorate

Seek out a container that's roomy enough to fit all the elements of this super-sweet kit.

A ready-to-assemble gingerbread house is sure to be a big hit with adults and children alike. And with all the decorations and "glue" supplied, there's no excuse not to get making it straight away.

1 Make templates from card stock using the measurements on page 172.
2 Put the flour, baking soda, ginger, and butter into a food processor. Whiz to form fine bread crumbs. Tip into a bowl and stir in the sugar.
3 Add the syrup and egg to the flour mixture and bring together with a flat-bladed knife until it forms clumps. Bring together with your hands to make a ball, then knead on a lightly floured counter until smooth. Shape into a disc, wrap in plastic wrap, and chill for 20 minutes.
4 Divide the dough in half. Roll out the first half on a lightly floured counter to a thickness of ⅛ inch. Using the templates as a guide, cut out four of each shape, re-rolling the dough as necessary. Arrange on lightly greased cookie sheets. Chill for 20 minutes.
5 Preheat the oven to 375°F. Bake the gingerbread in a preheated oven for 8 to 10 minutes until golden. Neaten the edges while still warm, using the templates as a guide. Let set on the cookie sheet for a few minutes then transfer to wire racks to cool. The gingerbread keeps for up to three months.
To gift wrap: Line a box with waxed paper, put in the gingerbread shapes, with more layers of waxed paper. Decant the royal icing sugar into small cellophane bags; put the candies into cellophane bags and tie with ribbon or colorful twine.
To assemble: First, prepare the "glue" with the royal icing sugar and a few drops of water to make a mixture that's pipeable. Pipe a line of icing along the base of one of the side walls and fix upright onto a cake board. Pipe along the edge and base of a pointed end wall and fix to the side wall. Continue with the other side and end walls to form a box. Hold in place for a few minutes to allow the icing to set and glue the pieces together. Pipe icing along the top edges of the house and position the roof pieces in place. Decorate with the candies, fixing in place with more icing. Use more icing to pipe windows and doors, if you like.

ITALIAN KIT

Everyone loves Italian food, and this simple dinner kit will go down a treat. Just add some good-quality pasta and a generous lump of Parmesan to finish off the gift.

FOR THE BASIL PESTO:
PREPARATION: **15 minutes**
MAKES: *about 12oz*

1 small clove garlic
1 cup pine nuts toasted
2 cups basil leaves
3½oz Parmesan, grated
scant ⅔ cup to generous ¾ cup
  extra-virgin olive oil, plus extra
  for storing

1 Put all of the ingredients, except the oil, into a food processor or blender and blitz together until fairly smooth.
2 With the motor running, gradually add enough oil to make a slightly sloppy mixture. Taste to check the seasoning.
3 Pour the pesto into sterilized jars, cover with a thin layer of oil, and seal. This vibrant paste keeps for up to two weeks in the fridge.

FOR THE BASIL OIL:
PREPARATION: **10 minutes,**
  plus standing
MAKES: *2½ cups*

large handful basil leaves and
  stalks, lightly bruised
2½ cups olive oil

1 Put the ingredients into a large bowl or jar, making sure that the herbs are submerged. Cover and let infuse in a cool, dark place for two weeks to a month.
2 Strain the oil into sterilized bottles, seal, and label. This oil keeps for six months in a cool, dark place.

FOR THE TAPENADE:
PREPARATION: **15 minutes**
MAKES: *about 10½oz*

1 large clove garlic, chopped
1⅔ cups pitted black olives
4 tbsp capers, drained and rinsed
8 anchovy fillets, roughly
  chopped
finely grated zest 1 lemon
2–3 tbsp extra-virgin olive oil

1 Whiz all of the ingredients, except the oil, in a food processor to make a coarse paste. Stir in enough olive oil to loosen.
2 Transfer into sterilized jars, seal, and label. This savory paste keeps for a month in the fridge.

Cute marshmallows and cinnamon-stick stirrers make this foodie kit much more than the sum of its parts.

HOT CHOCOLATE KIT

PREPARATION: *20 minutes*
MAKES: *6 sachets*

4 tbsp unsweetened cocoa powder
7 tbsp superfine sugar
generous ⅓ cup semisweet chocolate chips

TO COMPLETE THE GIFT:
mini marshmallows
cinnamon sticks

A perfect gift for when the nights draw in and the fire goes on—friends and family will thank you from the bottom of their slippersocks.

1 Mix together the cocoa and sugar until well combined. Stir in the chocolate chips. Divide among six sachets (3 tsp in each) and seal.
2 To complete the gift, tuck a few sachets of the hot chocolate mix into a mug of your choosing along with a jar of mini marshmallows and a few cinnamon sticks tied with a ribbon. Write the instructions on a tag.
To make a mug of hot chocolate: Tip the contents of one sachet into your mug. Heat generous ¾ cup of milk until piping hot, whisking often, then pour into the mug and stir with a cinnamon stick. Top with marshmallows and a spoonful of whipped cream, if you like.

SPICE BOX

FOR THE GARAM MASALA:
PREPARATION:
   10 minutes
MAKES: 3 tbsp

4 tbsp cardamom pods (or 1 tbsp cardamom seeds)
1 cinnamon stick, broken into pieces
2 tbsp coriander seeds
4 tsp black peppercorns
2 tsp whole cloves

Remove the seeds from the cardamom and discard the pods. Grind the spices to a powder in an electric coffee grinder, a spice mill, or a pestle and mortar. This mild blend for creamy curries keeps for up to two months.

FOR THE CHINESE FIVE SPICE:
PREPARATION:
   10 minutes
MAKES: 4 tbsp plus 1 tsp

12 star anise
2 tbsp Sichuan pepper
2 tbsp fennel seeds
4 tsp whole cloves
1 cinnamon stick, broken into pieces

Grind the spices to a powder in an electric coffee grinder, a spice mill, or a pestle and mortar. This mix is great for seasoning meat and poultry or in stir-fries and keeps for up to two months.

FOR THE ZA'ATAR:
PREPARATION:
   10 minutes
COOKING: 3 minutes
MAKES: 5 tbsp plus 2 tsp

generous ½ cup sesame seeds
4 tbsp sumac
5 tsp dried thyme

Dry roast the sesame seeds in a small skillet for a few minutes over medium-low heat until they smell nutty. Cool, then mix with the sumac and thyme until thoroughly combined. Stir into yogurt for a dip or sprinkle on kebabs before cooking. This spice mix keeps for two months.

FOR THE MIXED SPICE:
PREPARATION:
   10 minutes
MAKES: 4 tbsp plus 2 tsp

1 cinnamon stick, broken into pieces
2 tbsp whole allspice
2 tbsp coriander seeds
4 tsp whole cloves
4 blades of mace
2 tsp ground ginger
4 tsp grated nutmeg

Grind the spices to a powder in an electric coffee grinder, a spice mill, or a pestle and mortar. This is a wonderful spice for baking and keeps for up to two months.

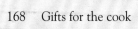

FOR THE CAJUN SEASONING:

PREPARATION:
10 minutes

MAKES: **3 tbsp plus 1 tsp**

5 tsp hot paprika
1 tsp ground black pepper
2 tsp each cayenne pepper and ground cumin
1 tsp dried oregano
1 tsp dried thyme

Mix together all the ingredients until thoroughly combined. This seasoning is great to rub on fish, meat, or poultry before grilling and keeps for up to two months.

A pleasing gift for novices or keen cooks who love to experiment with new flavors.

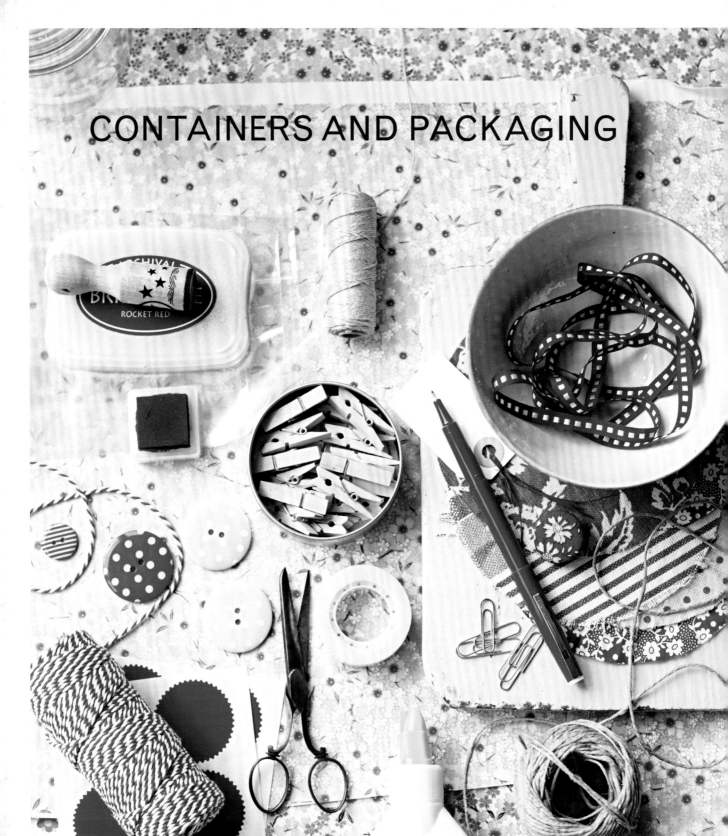

CONTAINERS AND PACKAGING

The fun for me doesn't stop with creating the food gifts themselves. I always keep an eye out for unusual wrappings and trimmings. I store these in a large box that I love to rummage through when the food is ready to package. The contents range from the mundane but indispensable items, such as waxed paper and cellophane for lining tins and boxes, to the flourishes of ribbons, string, ink stamps, buttons, and tags.

Don't forget an interesting container can be part of the gift, too: once eaten, a beautiful jar that contained chutney can be used for kitchen storage while a pretty tin emptied of cookies or chocolates becomes a keepsake box to admire.

Vintage fairs, thrift stores, and antique centers are rich hunting grounds for unusual packaging. Usually cheap to buy, they'll be a unique way of presenting a gift and can be tailored to the recipient's taste or interests. Be inventive: a pretty cup and saucer can be filled with sweets while a cake can be presented on a beautiful antique stand. Whatever you choose, have fun!

GINGERBREAD HOUSE TEMPLATES

Use the measurements below to make your own templates for the pieces of gingerbread.

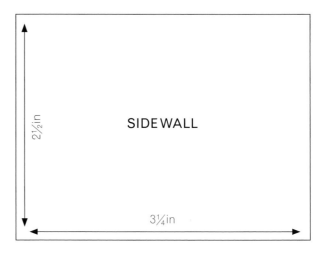

SIDE WALL

2½in

3¼in

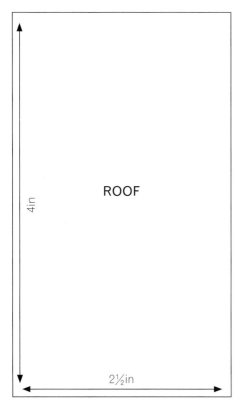

ROOF

4in

2½in

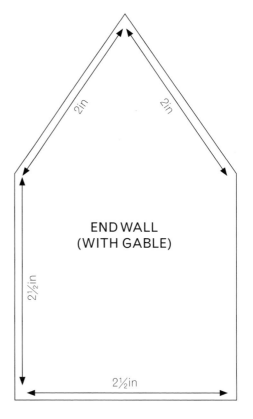

2in   2in

END WALL
(WITH GABLE)

2½in

2½in

RESOURCE SECTION

AMAZON

For all things related to baking and cooking, including a good selection of food coloring pastes and extracts, baking pans, kitchen and decorating equipment, and paper liners. It also has boxes, cellophane, strings, tapes, and paper tags for packaging ideas. www.amazon.com

SHOP BAKERS NOOK.COM

This online shop has an extensive range of bakeware, containers, decorations, and equipment. www.shopbakersnook.com 734-429-1320

HOBBY LOBBY

This crafty website—with stores nationwide—has an expansive section for baking and all manner of party supplies, which double as containers and packaging. www.shop.hobbylobby.com

GLOBAL SUGAR ART

As well as frostings, colors, and all manner of cake pans, this online store has a wonderful range of edible sprinkles, molds, cookie cutters, and gift boxes to choose from. www.globalsugarart.com 800-420-6088

MARTHA STEWART

For a million and one ideas for creative packaging and memorable gifts, as well as bakeware, utensils, and equipment. Many of her products are available nationwide at other stores, such as The Home Depot, Macy's, and Staples. www.shop.marthastewart.com

MICHAELS

These national craft stores are sure to have the baking, decorating, and packaging items you'll need. www.michaels.com

ULTIMATE BAKE

Everything you could ever need for making, baking, and decorating. storecooksdream.com 866-285-2665

ETSY

This massive site hosts myriad online shops selling cookie cutters, beautiful paper liners, cupcake cases, packaging for fun and unique gifts. It also sells vintage items if your searches in thrift stores have yielded little. www.etsy.com

EBAY

Items of all types can be sourced from the comfort of your home at eBay, so if you're looking for a vintage tea cup set, cellophane bags, ribbons, or shaped cookie cutters, you're bound to find something to fit the bill. ebay.com

MODERNIST PANTRY

For gelatin leaves and flavorings. www.modernistpantry.com 469-443-6634

THE GREAT AMERICAN SPICE CO.

Spices and flavorings galore at this online store. www.americanspice.com 877-677-4239

THE SPICE HOUSE

Spices, herbs, and seasonings; a great range of vanillas as well as plain glass jars. www.thespicehouse.com

SPECIALTY BOTTLE

There's more than a great range of bottles here, including some great round tins as seen on Martha Stewart, and you can buy as few as one at a time. www.specialtybottle.com 206-382-1100

INDEX

ACKNOWLEDGMENTS

I would like to thank the following people for their help with this book:

Tara Fisher for her stunning photography and **Caroline Reeves** for the creative and beautiful propping. You are both a joy to work with.

The team at Jacqui Small: **Penny Stock, Jo Copestick**, and, particularly, **Nikki Sims**, a brilliant and thorough editor who always asks the right questions.

The team at *Country Living* magazine—for being my official recipe tasters.

Most of all, my husband, **Keith**, for patiently ignoring and never complaining about the stacks of chutneys, pickles, and jellies, and tins of cookies, candies, and cakes that took over our kitchen for more than six months… Thank you.

The publisher would also like to thank **Caroline Arber** for the photographs on the following pages: 28, 44–45, 59, 114–115, 118–119, 126, 135, 158–159; all other photographs by **Tara Fisher**.

ABOUT THE AUTHOR

Alison Walker is the Food & Drink Editor of *Country Living* magazine in the UK. After gaining experience in editorial magazine publishing, she retrained as a professional chef at Leith's School of Food and Wine in London, UK, and graduated as Student of the Year in 2002. She then worked as a food stylist on various television programs and movie sets, such as the James Bond film, *Die Another Day*. Since then, Alison has worked as food editor on various glossy women's magazines in London. Immediately before joining *Country Living* magazine, she was Head of Cookery at *Good Housekeeping* (UK).